ATLANTA IN 100 OBJECTS

med my heart as
t only to me but to the
outh, the nation and its
ormer generations and
unity where all differences
rmony with the principles of
nts of our Judeo-Christian
Sincerely yours,
Martin Luther King, Jr.

Crackers
2

WE WILL PROVE OURSELVES MEN
127th REGt. U.S. COLORED TROOPS

WILLIAMS ST.
PEACHTREE

Atlanta in 100 Objects

A Century of Stories

ATLANTA
HISTORY
CENTER

In association with Scala Arts Publishers, Inc.

Acknowledgments

Atlanta History Center gratefully acknowledges the donors of the past 100 years for their support of the mission to preserve our history.

9,100 donors

17,500 donations

56,000 museum objects

38,000 library books

17,000 linear feet of archival documents (more than 3 miles)

42,000 plants

2,400 species

3,000 trees

Assorted chickens, sheep, goats, turkeys, salamanders, and bees

Any project, such as *Atlanta in 100 Objects*, is a team endeavor. We thank the many individuals who worked together to celebrate the centennial of Atlanta History Center.

We are indebted to Amy Durrell and Lisa Flaherty for laying the groundwork through research, interpretive ideas, and the initial writing for nearly all 100 essays. For a publication in which the objects are heroes, the photography is a principal component—our thanks to Mark Hill for the look, the vision, and the eye to see old stuff in a striking way.

The team at Atlanta History Center was composed of staff from a variety of departments and specialties, headed by Pola Changnon, and each involved with the professionalism that marks the preservation and study of collection objects—Lucy Abell, Erica Hague, Claire Haley, Jena Jones, Ammiel Lewis, John Schmidt, and Sue VerHoef. We also recognize those outside of our four walls for their contributions, including Helen Matthews and Rod Smith.

Special thanks to Timothy Frilingos as project manager and Michael Rose as publication manager.

And thank you to the thousands of supporters and stakeholders of Atlanta History Center for the first 100 years of arousing "in the friends and citizens of Atlanta an interest in its history."

Contents

Introduction

F. Sheffield Hale, President and CEO,
Atlanta History Center

You can tell a lot about a person by what they keep in their house.

Museums are similar. Through exhibitions, museums display collections of artifacts, photographs, letters, books, and more—the evidence of everyday life and stories about our past, present, and future. Behind exhibitions are thousands of additional objects that could not possibly all be displayed at once, but form the bedrock of the institution's resources and expertise.

This book contains 100 objects from Atlanta History Center's extensive collections, including the map Union troops used to prepare for the Battle of Atlanta and the calling card of General William T. Sherman, the land deed for the property containing the Muscogee site Standing Peachtree and the first map of Atlanta, folk art and fine art, dresses and shoes, football field–sized paintings and small sketches, and an honest-to-goodness carpetbag. The objects cover a wide range of history. Each can tell many stories.

Through these pages, objects tell the story of a city of complexity. Born at the humble beginning of a not-yet-existent railroad, evolved into the industrial engine behind a devastating war to secede from the United States, and hosting the beating heart of a movement toward equal rights for people of all races, Atlanta has seen a lot of history. Known as both the Black Mecca and the birthplace of *Gone With the Wind*, Atlanta encapsulates contradictions that seem incompatible but are inherent in the history of the entire nation.

In these pages are the story of a city, but more than that, the story of a city's chronicler. Founded in 1926, the Atlanta Historical Society began as a club of tight-knit Atlantans interested in the history of their young city, passionate about growing their knowledge, and sharing it with each other. Contained in the organization's stated mission was to "arouse in the citizens and friends of Atlanta an interest in its history."

The first artifact collected by the Society was in 1927: a set of pamphlets from Spelman College, a historically Black college in Atlanta. These pamphlets began a long tradition of collecting and preserving items of historical and cultural significance so that future generations would have access to and learn from them. The Society also preserved historic properties and landscapes on its campus, including the 1928 Swan House, and Smith Farm and Wood Cabin, both of which date from the 1840s. The institution benefited greatly from the work of the City of Atlanta's official historian, Franklin Garrett, who left volumes of research and memories

of the locally famous "Stump Franklin" nights, in which the public attempted to ask him a question about Atlanta history he did not know. They rarely succeeded.

In 1990, the institution became Atlanta History Center and continued a path of rapid growth with a new museum building. Now, after 100 years, the institution includes campuses in Buckhead and Midtown; 33 acres of curated gardens that contain extensive living collections of plants and animals; the world's most comprehensive Civil War collection under one roof; and one of the largest archives and collections in the southeastern United States, particularly strong in architecture, Southern history, maps, railroads, and textiles. From official City of Atlanta records to oral histories of veterans and families, the collections of Atlanta History Center strive to reflect the full, complicated history of the city we call home as the city continues to change and grow.

At the 100-year point, it is important to pause and reflect on what has been accomplished. Within these pages are 100 examples of the numerous stories that can be told about our collective past, different perspectives, and insights that, in turn, help inform our city's future.

This is Atlanta in 100 Objects.

ideas.
Congress.

Foreword

The Honorable Andrew Young
Former Mayor of Atlanta, U.S. Ambassador to the United Nations, and Member of the U.S. House of Representatives

For years, I've been caught up in the vision of Atlanta and what it can be.

I came to Atlanta in 1961. After starting my time in Georgia in small towns close to the Florida border, my wife and I spent four years in New York City. We came to Atlanta because she made herself clear: she didn't want to live in New York. It wasn't that she disliked New York, exactly—she loved the South.

I'm a preacher at heart, and I think Atlanta is a spiritual story. At that time, it was like God laid his hand on this plot of ground and was going to get all of his people moving together in the same direction. To me, the Atlanta Way was embodied in leaders from different backgrounds sitting together as brothers, planning out the future, because, as Martin Luther King Jr. said, they'd rather live as brothers and thrive than perish together as fools. It was a commitment to peace and prosperity.

The Atlanta story transcends politics, economics, race, and geography.

We need to understand why we have different opinions and how to find the things we have in common in spite of our differences. Atlanta History Center shows us that we can't create our future unless we understand our past. Every time I visit, I'm challenged to remember and re-experience the past, and learn something I couldn't learn anywhere else. Atlanta History Center helps us see in simple artifacts that our predecessor's visions really did exist, affirming another phrase often repeated by Dr. King: "If we can conceive it and believe it, we can achieve it."

This is a history center for the future.

Andrew Young's Congressional Campaign
Andrew Young with his father, Andrew Young Sr., election night, November 7, 1972
Boyd Lewis Photographs, Kenan Research Center at Atlanta History Center, VIS 101.576.026

Spelman College Bulletins

A gathering of 11 students and two teachers marked the beginning of Spelman College for women, founded in 1881 as Atlanta Baptist Female Seminary. One of those teachers remembered the donated space in the basement of the Friendship Baptist Church as dingy, but the women's goals were clear: "To be able to read their Bibles and to read and answer the letters from their children." In a few years, the school grew and moved to its current campus in southwest Atlanta, now home to more than 2,500 undergraduate students.

In the years following the Civil War, the promise of education drew free Black people, both recently emancipated and previously free, to Atlanta. Options for education included Atlanta University, founded in 1865; Morehouse College, founded in 1867; Clark College, founded in 1869; and Morris Brown College, founded in 1881.

These schools and others benefited from the support of Black churches, the growing number of educated Black residents in the city, and Northern philanthropy. Today, four schools with roots in these institutions form the Atlanta University Center, sharing resources and continuing to attract young Black students to Atlanta.

Together, these schools have educated leaders in politics, the arts, business, and other professions in Atlanta and nationwide. Students and graduates from these schools had a major role in leading the Civil Rights Movement. In the early 1960s, they led the Atlanta Student Movement, a series of organized nonviolent demonstrations that helped desegregate Atlanta.

Following the founding of Atlanta History Center in 1926, these programs were the first objects donated to the organization's collections.

Annual Academic Bulletins
Atlanta: Spelman College, 1888–1927
Gift of Lucy Hale Tapley, 1927

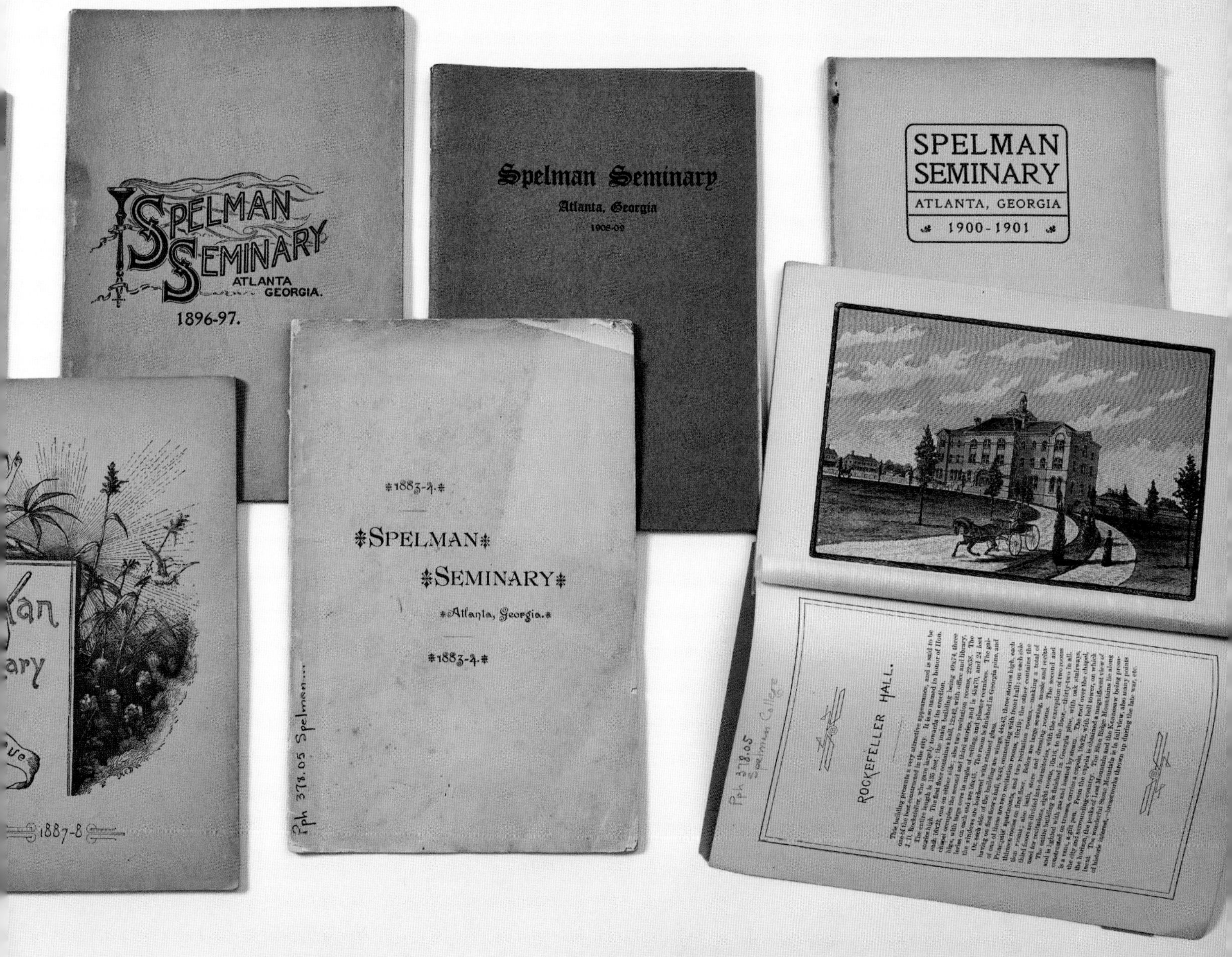
SPELMAN SEMINARY
ATLANTA GEORGIA.
1896-97.
Spelman Seminary
Atlanta, Georgia
1908-09
SPELMAN SEMINARY
ATLANTA, GEORGIA
1900-1901
1883-4.
SPELMAN
SEMINARY
Atlanta, Georgia.
1883-4.
Pph 378.05 Spelman...
1887-8
ROCKEFELLER HALL.

Peachtree Street

The name of Atlanta's best-known street connects the modern city to the Native people who lived here before white settlement. The nearest Muscogee settlement to modern-day Atlanta was a village called Pakanahuili, a name that translates to Standing Peachtree. The first written reference to the village appears in a Revolutionary War letter written in 1782 by Patriot Colonel John Daniel. Daniel mentions a rendezvous of Coweta Muscogee men "at Standing Peach Tree."

During the War of 1812, the Muscogee allied with the British and Georgia constructed a fort at Standing Peachtree to monitor nearby Muscogee settlements. The road built to connect nearby Fort Daniel in modern-day Gwinnett County with Fort Standing Peachtree was the first "Peachtree Road." The road ran from the base of Hog Mountain to what is now the site of Atlanta's water reclamation plant. Later, the name was given to the street running right through the heart of Atlanta—Peachtree Street.

In the 1930s, Margaret Mitchell's novel *Gone With the Wind* brought Peachtree Street into popular culture, leading to its global recognition as Atlanta's "Main Street," which contributed to its popularity. It also fueled Atlantans' desire to have an address on Peachtree.

Developers and city planners have thus provided variations on the original, often increasing wayfinding confusion: Peachtree Lane, Peachtree Avenue, Peachtree Circle, Peachtree Drive, Peachtree Road, Peachtree Walk, Peachtree Way, Peachtree Battle Avenue, and more. There are more than 70 streets with some form of Peachtree in their name in Metropolitan Atlanta.

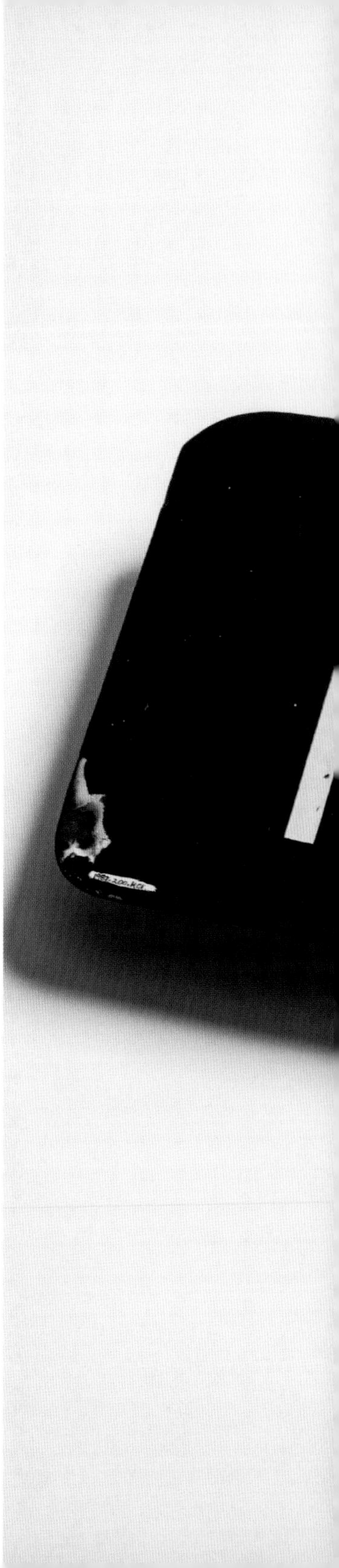

Street Sign
City of Atlanta, circa 1930
Gift of Harvey Brickley, 1987

WILLIAMS ST.
EACHTREE ST.

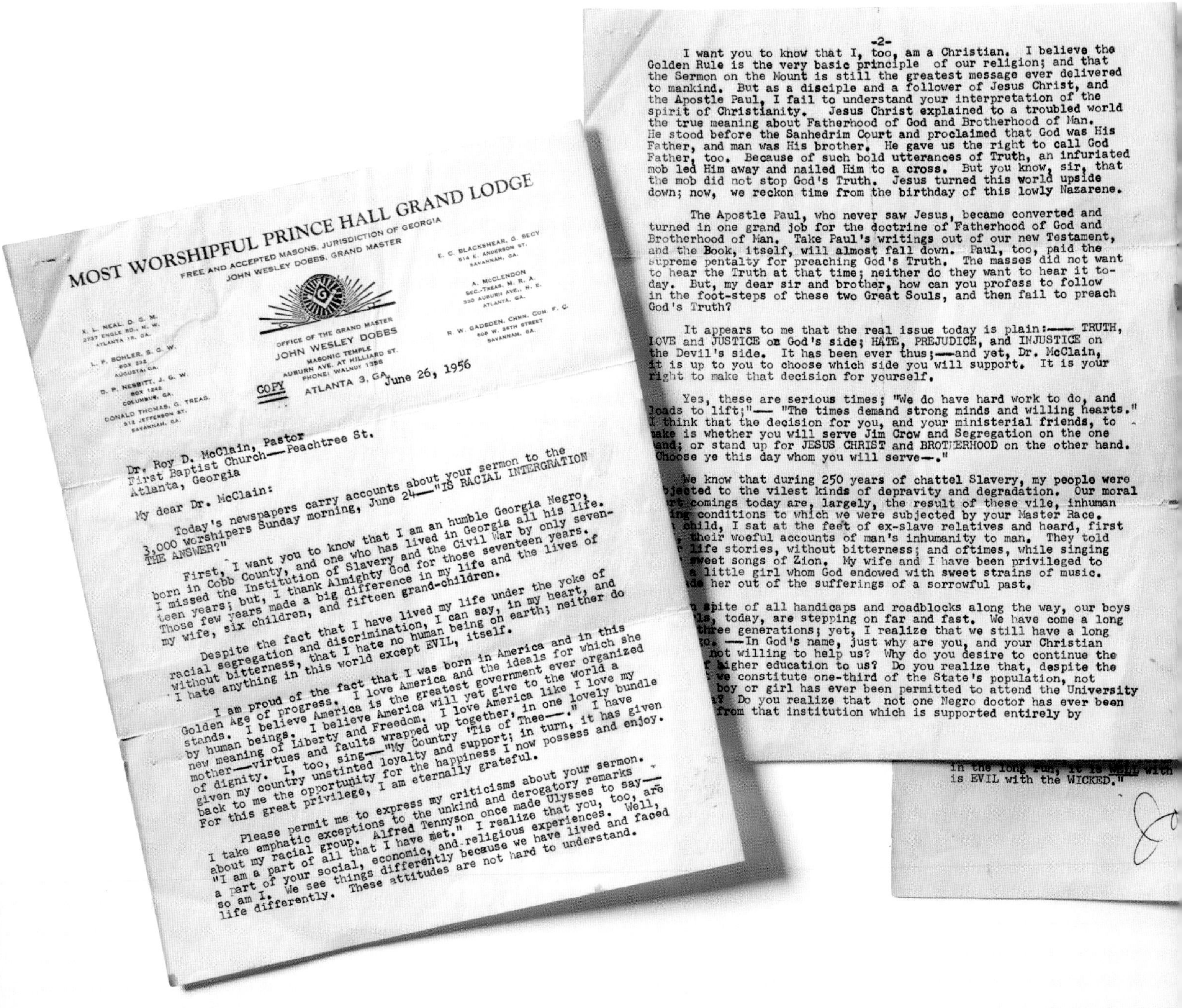

MOST WORSHIPFUL PRINCE HALL GRAND LODGE
FREE AND ACCEPTED MASONS, JURISDICTION OF GEORGIA
JOHN WESLEY DOBBS, GRAND MASTER

X. L. NEAL, D. G. M.
2737 ENGLE RD., N. W.
ATLANTA 18, GA.

L. P. BOHLER, S. G. W.
BOX 232
AUGUSTA, GA.

D. P. NESBITT, J. G. W.
BOX 1242
COLUMBUS, GA.

DONALD THOMAS, G. TREAS.
512 JEFFERSON ST.
SAVANNAH, GA.

OFFICE OF THE GRAND MASTER
JOHN WESLEY DOBBS
MASONIC TEMPLE
AUBURN AVE. AT HILLIARD ST.
PHONE: WALNUT 1358
ATLANTA 3, GA.

E. C. BLACKSHEAR, G. SECY
514 E. ANDERSON ST.
SAVANNAH, GA.

A. McCLENDON
SEC.-TREAS. M. R. A.
330 AUBURN AVE., N. E.
ATLANTA, GA.

R. W. GADSDEN, CHMN. COM. F. C.
608 W. 36TH STREET
SAVANNAH, GA.

COPY

June 26, 1956

Dr. Roy D. McClain, Pastor
First Baptist Church—Peachtree St.
Atlanta, Georgia

My dear Dr. McClain:

Today's newspapers carry accounts about your sermon to the 3,000 worshipers Sunday morning, June 24—"IS RACIAL INTERGRATION THE ANSWER?"

First, I want you to know that I am an humble Georgia Negro, born in Cobb County, and one who has lived in Georgia all his life. I missed the Institution of Slavery and the Civil War by only seventeen years; but, I thank Almighty God for those seventeen years. Those few years made a big difference in my life and the lives of my wife, six children, and fifteen grand-children.

Despite the fact that I have lived my life under the yoke of racial segregation and discrimination, I can say, in my heart, and without bitterness, that I hate no human being on earth; neither do I hate anything in this world except EVIL, itself.

I am proud of the fact that I was born in America and in this Golden Age of progress. I love America and the ideals for which she stands. I believe America is the greatest government ever organized by human beings. I believe America will yet give to the world a new meaning of Liberty and Freedom. I love America like I love my mother—virtues and faults wrapped up together, in one lovely bundle of dignity. I, too, sing—"My Country 'Tis of Thee—." I have given my country unstinted loyalty and support; in turn, it has given back to me the opportunity for the happiness I now possess and enjoy. For this great privilege, I am eternally grateful.

Please permit me to express my criticisms about your sermon. I take emphatic exceptions to the unkind and derogatory remarks about my racial group. Alfred Tennyson once made Ulysses to say—"I am a part of all that I have met." I realize that you, too, are a part of your social, economic, and religious experiences. Well, so am I. We see things differently because we have lived and faced life differently. These attitudes are not hard to understand.

-2-

I want you to know that I, too, am a Christian. I believe the Golden Rule is the very basic principle of our religion; and that the Sermon on the Mount is still the greatest message ever delivered to mankind. But as a disciple and a follower of Jesus Christ, and the Apostle Paul, I fail to understand your interpretation of the spirit of Christianity. Jesus Christ explained to a troubled world the true meaning about Fatherhood of God and Brotherhood of Man. He stood before the Sanhedrim Court and proclaimed that God was His Father, and man was His brother. He gave us the right to call God Father, too. Because of such bold utterances of Truth, an infuriated mob led Him away and nailed Him to a cross. But you know, sir, that the mob did not stop God's Truth. Jesus turned this world upside down; now, we reckon time from the birthday of this lowly Nazarene.

The Apostle Paul, who never saw Jesus, became converted and turned in one grand job for the doctrine of Fatherhood of God and Brotherhood of Man. Take Paul's writings out of our new Testament, and the Book, itself, will almost fall down. Paul, too, paid the supreme pentalty for preaching God's Truth. The masses did not want to hear the Truth at that time; neither do they want to hear it today. But, my dear sir and brother, how can you profess to follow in the foot-steps of these two Great Souls, and then fail to preach God's Truth?

It appears to me that the real issue today is plain:— TRUTH, LOVE and JUSTICE on God's side; HATE, PREJUDICE, and INJUSTICE on the Devil's side. It has been ever thus;—and yet, Dr. McClain, it is up to you to choose which side you will support. It is your right to make that decision for yourself.

Yes, these are serious times; "We do have hard work to do, and loads to lift;"— "The times demand strong minds and willing hearts." I think that the decision for you, and your ministerial friends, to make is whether you will serve Jim Crow and Segregation on the one hand; or stand up for JESUS CHRIST and BROTHERHOOD on the other hand. Choose ye this day whom you will serve—."

We know that during 250 years of chattel Slavery, my people were ...bjected to the vilest kinds of depravity and degradation. Our moral ...rt comings today are, largely, the result of these vile, inhuman ...ing conditions to which we were subjected by your Master Race. ... child, I sat at the feet of ex-slave relatives and heard, first ..., their woeful accounts of man's inhumanity to man. They told ... life stories, without bitterness; and oftimes, while singing ... sweet songs of Zion. My wife and I have been privileged to ... a little girl whom God endowed with sweet strains of music. ...de her out of the sufferings of a sorrowful past.

...n spite of all handicaps and roadblocks along the way, our boys ...ls, today, are stepping on far and fast. We have come a long ... three generations; yet, I realize that we still have a long ...go. —In God's name, just why are you, and your Christian ... not willing to help us? Why do you desire to continue the ... higher education to us? Do you realize that, despite the ... we constitute one-third of the State's population, not ... boy or girl has ever been permitted to attend the University ...a? Do you realize that not one Negro doctor has ever been ... from that institution which is supported entirely by

in the long run, it is WELL with
is EVIL with the WICKED."

Civil Rights Correspondence

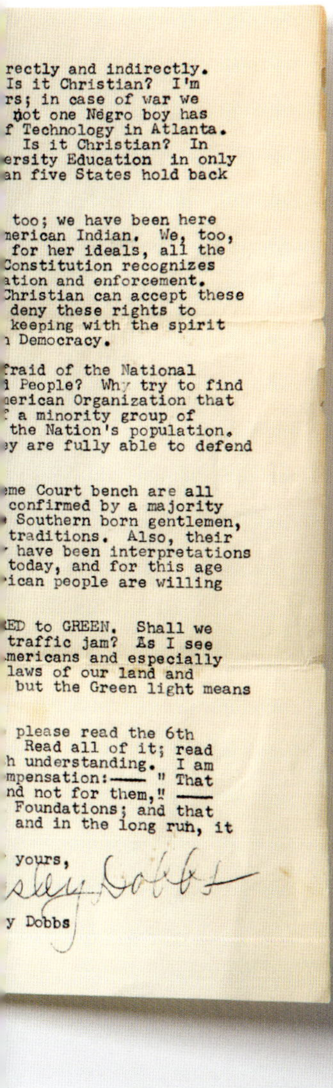
rectly and indirectly.
Is it Christian? I'm
rs; in case of war we
not one Negro boy has
f Technology in Atlanta.
Is it Christian? In
ersity Education in only
an five States hold back

too; we have been here
merican Indian. We, too,
for her ideals, all the
Constitution recognizes
ation and enforcement.
Christian can accept these
deny these rights to
keeping with the spirit
n Democracy.

fraid of the National
d People? Why try to find
merican Organization that
f a minority group of
the Nation's population.
ey are fully able to defend

eme Court bench are all
confirmed by a majority
Southern born gentlemen,
traditions. Also, their
have been interpretations
today, and for this age
rican people are willing

ED to GREEN. Shall we
traffic jam? As I see
mericans and especially
laws of our land and
but the Green light means

please read the 6th
Read all of it; read
h understanding. I am
mpensation:— " That
nd not for them," —
Foundations; and that
and in the long run, it

yours,

y Dobbs

In June 1956 after a federal district court declared segregated public buses unconstitutional, Dr. Roy McClain, pastor of the First Baptist Church of Atlanta, delivered a sermon. McClain led one of the South's largest white Baptist churches, and on that day he spoke against integration: "Our yards are not as clean as we want them to be, but we steadfastly resent those who come to sweep our yards for us. Time is judgment enough upon us and with the patience and intelligence of God's guidance we will sweep."

Black civic leader John Wesley Dobbs responded. Dobbs had long worked for racial equality in segregated Atlanta. This stationery reflects his leadership as lifetime Grand Master in the fraternal organization of the Prince Hall Masons. His record of success included founding the Atlanta Negro Voters League; lobbying for hiring the first Black police officers; and installing streetlights on Auburn Avenue, which was the center of the city's Black community. Commonly known as the unofficial "Mayor" of Auburn Avenue, Dobbs was always willing to take on a challenge.

Dobbs asked McClain to act as a Christian and as an American:

> Colored people are American Citizens, too; we have been here just as long as anybody else, except the American Indian. We, too, helped build America. . . . Please tell me, then kind sir, just how a Christian can accept these rights for himself and at the same time, deny these rights to his fellow-man? To do so, would not be in keeping with the spirit of Jesus Christ, nor the spirit of American Democracy.

John Wesley Dobbs to Dr. Roy McClain
June 26, 1956
Gift of Sheffield Hale, 2021

Izzy

Atlanta introduced its mascot for the 1996 Olympic Games at the closing ceremonies of the 1992 Olympics in Barcelona, Spain. Named "Whatizit," broadcasters struggled to describe it with the character generating more questions than excitement. Unlike previous Olympic mascots, Whatizit had no discernible connection to the host city—or to anything else.

Created by John Ryan of DESIGNefx and originally named "Hi-Rez," the mascot was intended to "break the mold" and push the boundaries of Computer Generated-Imagery (CGI animation), a technology then in its early stages. The shape was based on the teardrop, which, according to Ryan, "can convey emotion . . . it's provocative." Ryan added features to suggest a personality and to make it child-friendly, a requirement of the Atlanta Committee for the Olympic Games (ACOG).

ACOG believed the mascot would be uncontroversial and profitable. The committee had hoped for an Olympic Games that left Atlanta debt free, and merchandise featuring a cute mascot would be a part of that financial success.

The less-than-positive response, however, caused some second-guessing. ACOG decided a renaming would boost sales. Children around the world proposed new names, and those from Atlanta selected the final one. In October 1993, Whatizit became Izzy. Critics continued to lambast its nonspecific animated design, but a successful Atlanta icon was born.

Izzy
Atlanta Committee for the Olympic Games, 1996
Gift of Atlanta Committee for the Olympic Games, 2002

First Map of Atlanta

In 1851, Atlanta's city council hired civil engineer Edward A. Vincent to design a map to document and celebrate the growing Southern city. The proposed map was to present a circle, one mile in radius, marking the city limits, with the Western & Atlantic Railroad's Zero Milepost at the center. Vincent beautifully illustrated the curved lines that gave Atlanta streets their unusual layout.

The city of Atlanta in the 1850s was vibrant and bustling. The 1850 census records a population of 2,572 (including 2,060 white people, 493 enslaved people, and 19 free Black residents) with an average age of 35. Following Fulton County's creation in 1853, Atlanta became the county seat and began to lobby to become the new state capital of Georgia.

People arrived in Atlanta from all parts of the country and the wealthiest residents built homes on Alabama and South Forsyth Streets. A new food market and a free school were built to support the growing population. The citizens also put aside six acres for a graveyard, later to be expanded to 42 acres and named Oakland Cemetery. By far the most impactful investment by the new city was the completion of Union Station in 1853, also designed by Vincent, near present-day Five Points in downtown Atlanta.

During the American Civil War, Major General William T. Sherman's army adapted Vincent's map and provided it to troops preparing for the siege of Atlanta in July 1864. As prepared by the army's topographical office, the maps, like this one used by the Army of the Cumberland, were printed on linen, allowing for easy folding and preventing tears.

Atlanta
Drawn and printed at the Topographical Engineer Office, Army of the Cumberland in the field, July 25, 1864
Gift of John K. Hooper in memory of Elizabeth Kontz Hooper, 1998

ATLANTA
CORPORATION LINE
Alexander St
Simpson St
Buker St
Harris St
Cain St
Ellis St
Houston St
Wheat St
Green St
Stockton St
Markum St
Nelson St
Walker St
Peters St
Haynes St
Mangum St
STATE SQUARE
Decatur St
Collins St
Butler St
Pratt St
Fillmore St
Pearce St
Taylor St
Washington St
Yonge St
Ivy St
Peachtree St
Forsyth St
Pryor St
Lloyd St
Mitchell St
Fair St
Hunter St
Thompson St
Garnett St
Frazer Alley
Hill St
GEORGIA R.R.
White Hall
Scale 4 inches = 1 mile
From Vincent's Subdivision Map, published by the City Council.
INDEX:
STATE SQUARE. General Passenger Depot.
A. W. & A. R.R. Freight Warehouse
B. G. R.R. Locomotive House
C. G. R.R. Freight Warehouse
D. M.W. R.R. Locomotive House
E. M.W. R.R. Freight Warehouse
F. La Grange do do
1. Episcopal Church and Parsonage
2. Presbyterian Church
3. Baptist Church
4. 1st Methodist Ch. & Parsonage
5. 2d do do
6. Protestant Methodist Church
7. African do do
8. Christian Church
9. Free School
10. Union School
11. Haygood's Academy
12. Car Factory
13. Foundry
14. Thompson's Hotel
15. Lloyd's do
16. City do
17. Market House
18. Guard House
Drawn and printed at Topl. Engr Office, Hd.Qrs. A.C., in the field

Dave Drake Storage Jars

Dave belongs to Mr Miles / wher [sic] the
oven bakes & the pot biles [sic]
Dave Drake, 1840

David Drake was one of many enslaved laborers working in the ceramic workshops of Edgefield, South Carolina. It is believed he took the last name of the white slaveholder Harvey Drake, whose records show that he purchased Dave in about 1818. The paperwork notes that Dave was about 17 years old and "country born," meaning he was born in the U.S. and not Africa.

Dave Drake etched the wet clay of this small storage jar: "Feb 11/1852/Dave." Above the inscription are seven incised dots followed by two slash marks, indicating the jar's 7-gallon capacity. The larger 30-gallon jar is inscribed, "The fourth of July is surely come—to blow the fife and beat the drum." On the opposite side, Drake wrote: "LM July 4, 1859/ Dave." The "LM" stands for Lewis Miles, Drake's slaveholder at the time.

The inscriptions demonstrate that Drake was able to read and write, which was illegal for enslaved people in South Carolina. Beginning in 1834, Drake inscribed dates, proverbs, or short poems on some of the pots he crafted. He began signing his own name by 1840. In marking his work, Drake created a record of his life uncommon for enslaved people.

The size of Drake's pots also makes his work notable. He crafted pots more than two feet tall that held 40 gallons. The clay required to make pots this size weighed hundreds of pounds when wet, a testament to Drake's strength. Drake used a combination of techniques, including wheel throwing the bottom portion and then adding coils of clay by hand to build the height.

Remembered today as Dave the Potter, Drake worked as a potter for more than five decades, including his life after emancipation.

Storage Jar, 30 Gallons
Dave Drake, potter, Stony Bluff Manufactory, Edgefield District, South Carolina, 1859
Gift of Dr. John A. Burrison, 1995

Storage Jar, 7 Gallons
Dave Drake, potter, Stony Bluff Manufactory, Edgefield District, South Carolina, 1852
Gift of the Foreman Family in memory of James Crawford Foreman, 1995

The Atlanta Spirit

In his 1948 book *The Atlanta Spirit*, business leader Ivan Allen Sr. defined what set Atlanta apart from other cities:

> It is a city of cool nights; an equable all-the-year-round climate; good working conditions. . . . It is a city where the men walk fast . . . and work fast.

Allen defined Atlanta as a hardworking community with the drive to rebuild after destruction. Atlantans, he said, overcame a lack of traditional features that defined many American cities of the time and relied on modern assets, including "Railways! Highways! Airways!"

Allen founded a successful office supply company and invested his time and leadership in civic groups, including the Chamber of Commerce, Atlanta Convention & Visitors Bureau, and Rotary Club. In the 1920s, he led the city's Forward Atlanta campaign that brought approximately 750 new businesses, tens of thousands of jobs, and an estimated $34 million to the city's economy. His son Ivan Allen Jr. continued the commitment to civic duty by serving as Atlanta's mayor in the 1960s.

Allen Sr. also celebrated the city's transition away from the typical Southern agricultural economy: "With the steel shears of industry, [Atlanta] has cut the apron strings of cotton and branched out to make fuller and greater use of its natural resources and native talent and ability."

Allen was the quintessential booster, and exemplified the Atlanta Spirit—the ambitious, entrepreneurial, and resilient attitude that shaped the city's historical identity. The term embodies Atlanta's ability to reinvent itself and rise from the ashes of adversity, much like the Phoenix in the city's seal.

The Atlanta Spirit: Altitude + Attitude
Ivan Allen Sr., author
Atlanta: Ivan Allen-Marshall Company, 1948
Purchase with funds for the Collections, 2025

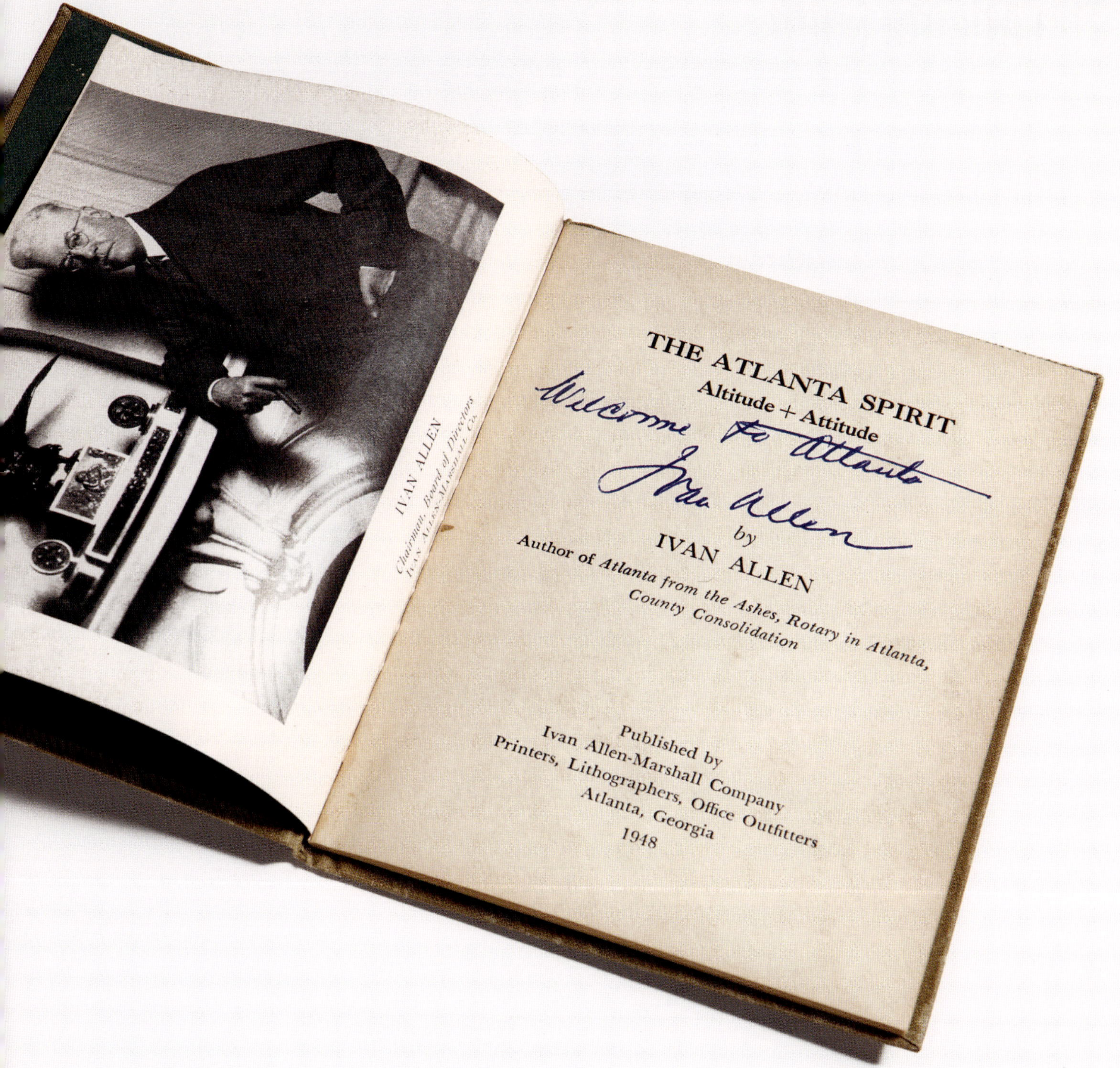
IVAN ALLEN
Chairman, Board of Directors
IVAN ALLEN-MARSHALL CO.
THE ATLANTA SPIRIT
Altitude + Attitude
Welcome to Atlanta
Ivan Allen
by
IVAN ALLEN
Author of Atlanta from the Ashes, Rotary in Atlanta, County Consolidation
Published by
Ivan Allen-Marshall Company
Printers, Lithographers, Office Outfitters
Atlanta, Georgia
1948

The Atlanta Journal
THE ATLANTA CONSTITUTION
Peachtree
Road Race
1980
NIKE
ATLANTA
TRACK CLUB

Peachtree Road Race T-shirt

> The road race was the one time this huge sprawling city of ours gets together, points in the same direction, and accomplishes something all together no matter what part of town you are from and who you are.
>
> Julia Emmons
> Former Director, Atlanta Track Club
> Former Trustee, Atlanta History Center

The Peachtree Road Race is a 10-kilometer race through the heart of Atlanta. On July 4, runners from all over the world come to take part. Participant numbers have grown steadily from 150 runners in 1970 to approximately 60,000 in 2025. The runners range from lauded professional athletes to first-time or veteran amateurs, many in pursuit of the one tangible benefit of the effort: a Peachtree Road Race T-shirt.

At the first race in 1970, the "Original 110" runners crossed the finish line in today's Woodruff Park in downtown Atlanta. That year, the winner was future 1972 Olympian, popular sports author, and Westminster Schools graduate Jeff Galloway. In 1972, Emory University faculty member Julia Emmons ran the race and finished second. Emmons went on to organize the road race for 22 years as director of the Atlanta Track Club.

The Peachtree Road Race T-shirt was introduced in 1971, though only the first 198 finishers received one. Soon, "winning" a T-shirt became a major incentive to push to the finish line. The Atlanta community's investment in the shirt became so great that after one unpopular design in 1994, an annual design contest was launched with the citizens of Atlanta choosing the winner.

The Peachtree Road Race, which the *Atlanta Journal-Constitution* began sponsoring in 1976, is now the largest 10k in the nation and a point of pride for tens of thousands of sweaty Atlantans.

Commemorative T-Shirt
Nike, Beaverton, Oregon, 1980
Gift of an anonymous donor, 1987

Moulthrop Bowl

The elegant simplicity of this turned wooden bowl reflects years of practice and innovation by Georgia artist Ed Moulthrop. As a teenager, Moulthrop was drawn to woodworking. When he was 15, he ordered a lathe through the mail and taught himself to use it, beginning a lifetime of experimentation. Trained as an architect, Moulthrop designed buildings and taught at the Georgia Institute of Technology, but his calling to woodworking led him to begin a full-time artistic career that spanned nearly 30 years.

While his early works were small, Moulthrop eventually tackled large pieces of wood. To do this, he forged his own tools. Moulthrop could turn logs weighing thousands of pounds, crafting vessels large enough to hold a person.

Moulthrop sought to highlight the natural grain and beauty of each piece of wood with which he worked and saw opportunity in logs others rejected as soft, rotted, or misshapen. A network of metro Atlanta tree trimmers brought him wood felled by storms or land clearing. Some vessels shone with bright colors created by bacteria that discolored the wood but hadn't damaged the tree. Others, made of partially rotted wood, were marked by striations.

As the contemporary craft movement rekindled interest in traditional handcrafts, Moulthrop brought an artist's eye and an innovative mind to woodturning, helping to raise craft into art.

This bowl was presented to Philip Trammell Shutze, architect of Atlanta History Center's Swan House, by Georgia Governor George Busbee in recognition of being named a recipient of the 1978 Governor's Awards in the Arts.

Moulthrop Bowl
Ed Moulthrop, artist,
Atlanta, 1978
Gift of Philip Trammell Shutze, 1978

Martin Luther King Jr. Letter

In 1964, the Rev. Dr. Martin Luther King Jr. received the Nobel Peace Prize for his work in the Civil Rights Movement and his nonviolent approach to securing the civil and voting rights of Black citizens. In segregated Atlanta, how—or if—to celebrate his award became controversial.

Behind the scenes, a group of progressive community leaders planned an event at the Dinkler Plaza Hotel in downtown Atlanta. Organizers included the Roman Catholic Archbishop of Atlanta Paul John Hallinan; Morehouse College President Benjamin Mays; Rabbi Jacob Rothschild; and newspaperman Ralph McGill, himself a Pulitzer Prize winner for editorials encouraging racial equality.

Atlanta's business community hesitated to honor a man whom many white leaders believed disrupted business and unsettled Southern traditions. Years earlier, city leaders promoted Atlanta as the City Too Busy to Hate, but after the Nobel Prize, they risked embarrassment if they failed to honor Dr. King's accomplishment.

The business community relented after an unflattering article highlighted their indecision in the *New York Times*. Support for the effort also came through the efforts of Mayor Ivan Allen Jr., who obtained help from retired Coca-Cola Company President Robert W. Woodruff and company President and CEO Paul Austin.

In January 1965, guests from the city's white and Black communities came together for the celebratory dinner. Atlanta Vice Mayor (and future mayor) Sam Massell Jr. later described the nervous tension in the room. Following an awkward start, the evening proceeded without incident and ended with a spontaneous sing-along of "We Shall Overcome" by attendees.

As president of the Southern Christian Leadership Conference, Dr. King and his staff coordinated civil rights activities across the South. Due to his organizing protests in Selma, Alabama, Dr. King did not send a thank-you letter until March 1965. The Selma protesters were beaten attempting to cross the Edmund Pettus Bridge, and the images of the event known as Bloody Sunday spurred support for the Civil Rights Movement across the nation.

334 Auburn Ave.,
Atlanta, Georgia
Telephone

Dr. Martin Luther King Jr. to Vice Mayor Sam Massell
March 15, 1965
Gift of Sam Massell Jr., 1991

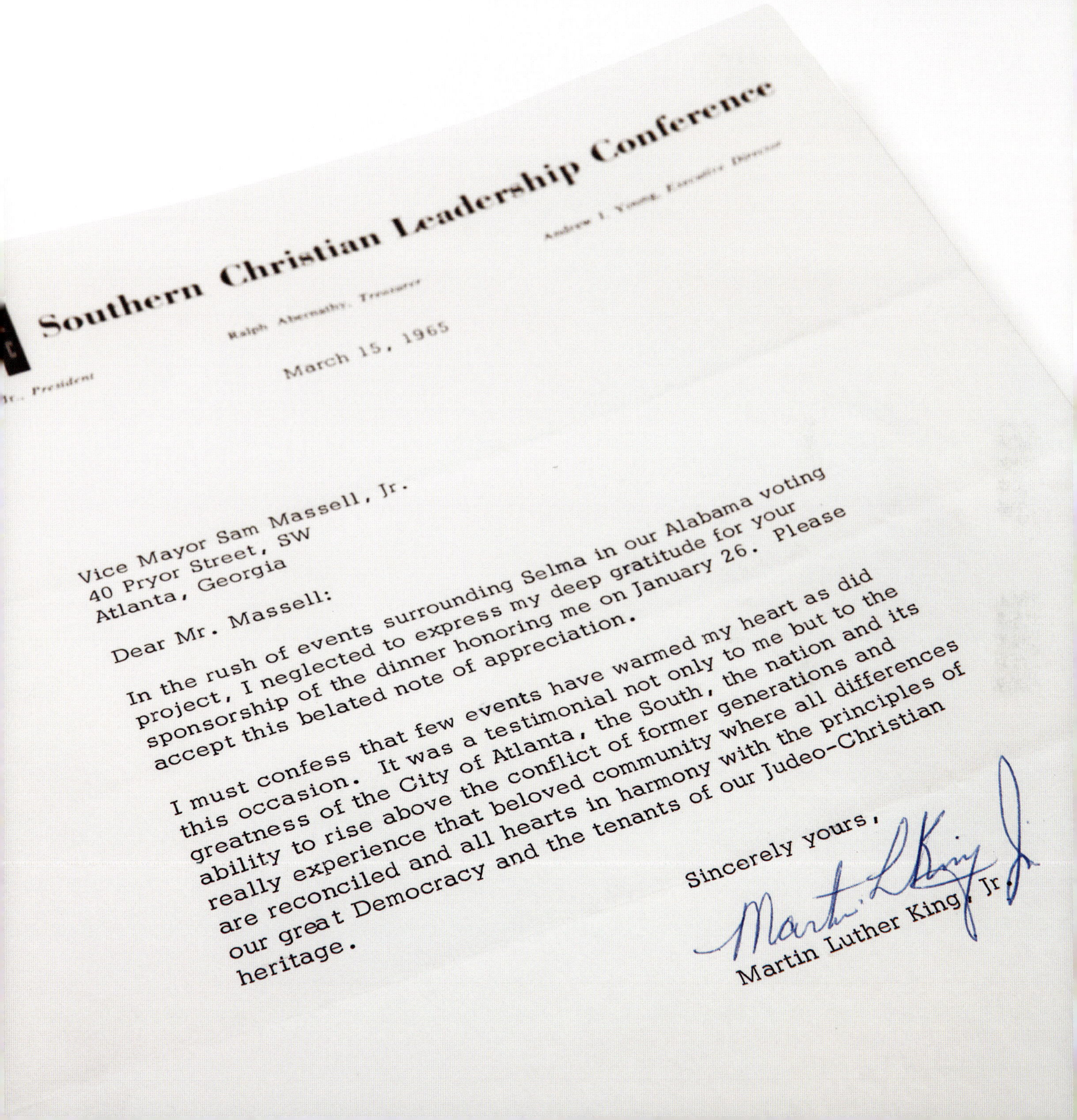

Southern Christian Leadership Conference

Jr., President — Ralph Abernathy, Treasurer — Andrew J. Young, Executive Director

March 15, 1965

Vice Mayor Sam Massell, Jr.
40 Pryor Street, SW
Atlanta, Georgia

Dear Mr. Massell:

In the rush of events surrounding Selma in our Alabama voting project, I neglected to express my deep gratitude for your sponsorship of the dinner honoring me on January 26. Please accept this belated note of appreciation.

I must confess that few events have warmed my heart as did this occasion. It was a testimonial not only to me but to the greatness of the City of Atlanta, the South, the nation and its ability to rise above the conflict of former generations and really experience that beloved community where all differences are reconciled and all hearts in harmony with the principles of our great Democracy and the tenants of our Judeo-Christian heritage.

Sincerely yours,

Martin L King Jr.

Martin Luther King, Jr.

FO

The Fox Theatre

The Fox Theatre marquee has brightened Peachtree Street since 1929. These letters, used from the 1950s until a digital marquee was installed in the 1990s, advertised the motion pictures and film stars that were seen by movie fans inside Atlanta's ornate movie palace.

In 1928, the Yaarab Temple Shriners proposed a building to provide its members with a place to gather. Atlanta architectural firm Marye, Alger & Vinour designed the ornate Moorish-, Egyptian-, and Turkish-themed building. While in the planning stages, an auditorium was suggested to accommodate non-Shriner events. Growing construction costs forced the Shriners to lease the auditorium to Fox Theatres Corporation, a national chain of grand silent-movie theaters.

Completed in 1929, the Fox Theatre was plagued by financial problems beginning with the Great Depression. The company Mosque Inc. was formed in 1935 to buy and manage the building. By the 1970s, however, movie palaces were closing, and in 1974 Mosque announced the planned demolition of the theater to make room for the headquarters of Southern Bell Telephone & Telegraph Company.

Two weeks later, a crowd of 2,500 gathered at the theater to form a plan to stop the demolition of the building. The "Save the Fox" campaign and its many volunteers secured funding, and a nonprofit organization, Atlanta Landmarks, was created to ensure the building's future, restore its architecture, and manage the theater's offerings. Today, the exquisitely restored Fox Theatre remains an important part of Atlanta's arts scene as a home to touring Broadway shows, popular music concerts, and the occasional movie.

Movie Marquee Letters
Unidentified maker, circa 1950
Gift of Atlanta Landmarks, 1995

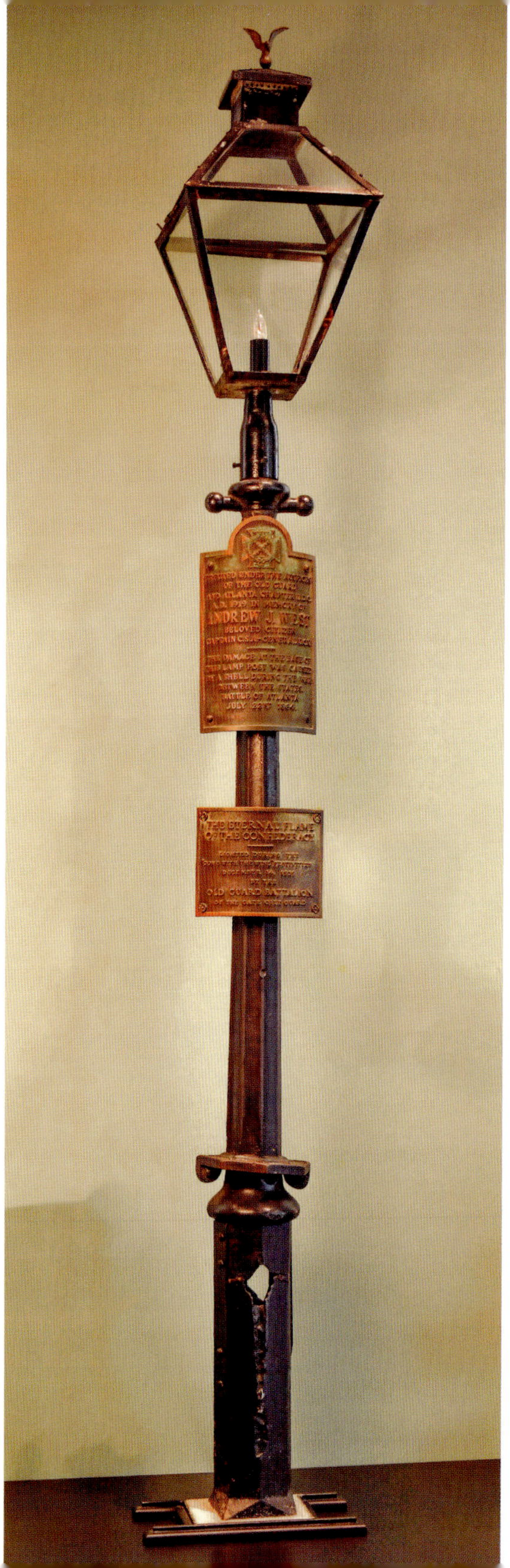

Lamppost
Atlanta Gas Light Company, 1855
Gift of City of Atlanta, 2017
The damage to the lamppost—with a hole through the base—was caused by a Union shell during the siege of Atlanta, August 1864.

Solomon and Nancy Luckie

Solomon Luckie, elegantly dressed in a waistcoat and jacket and wearing a gold ring on his finger, presents an image of a successful businessman in early Atlanta. He was part of the small population of free Black Atlantans living in the city before emancipation. From his downtown barbershop and bathhouse, Luckie rose to become one of Atlanta's wealthiest Black entrepreneurs.

For Luckie and the approximately 40 free Black or mixed-race people living in the city, life came with restrictions. In Atlanta, free people of color needed a white sponsor to move into the city. They also had to pay a fee and seek permission from the city council to engage in everyday activities, such as hosting visitors or starting businesses.

Luckie's odds-defying path to success was cut short during the U.S. Army's siege of Atlanta in the Civil War. In August 1864, Union forces bombarded the city with artillery. A shell burst near Luckie and shrapnel struck him as he leaned against a lamppost at Whitehall and Alabama Streets. Bystanders took Luckie to get medical help, but he died from blood loss.

Luckie's wife, Nancy, and their three children survived to see the end of the war and the abolishment of slavery. His descendants would live to see decades of success and struggles for Black Atlantans.

Today, the lamppost is exhibited at Atlanta History Center as an artifact related to the Cyclorama painting *The Battle of Atlanta*.

Nancy Cunningham Luckie and Solomon Luckie
Unidentified photographer, circa 1860
Gift of Julia and George Payne, 1986

The Atlanta Way

Following the Civil War and Reconstruction, Atlanta forged an aspirational identity as a "New South" city. Bound up in this aspiration was the inherent tension between forward progress and legalized segregation. Despite legal and social limitations resulting from this system, both Black and white community, business, and political leaders worked behind the scenes to achieve mutual goals. Over time, this process evolved into a set of practices collectively known as the Atlanta Way.

When asked about the Atlanta Way, U.N. Ambassador Andrew Young defined it as a process embodied by the Rev. Dr. Martin Luther King Jr.'s admonition that Atlantans could live together as brothers or perish together as fools. In early iterations, white politicians sought support from Black community leaders, who, although barred from holding office formally, wielded immense power through local institutions, such as churches and businesses, and through local bond referendums.

Later, following the end of segregation and the election of Maynard Jackson, the first Black mayor of Atlanta, the Atlanta Way took on a different tone. The city leadership consisted of Black Atlantans, though many major businesses continued to be run by white men. This letter from Charlie Loudermilk to then-Mayor Andrew Young embodies this new stage of the Atlanta Way, in which business and political leaders continued to meet behind the scenes to build trust and work together for the betterment of the city—and business.

Charlie Loudermilk to Mayor Andrew Young
January 18, 1982
Courtesy of the Russell Family, 2022

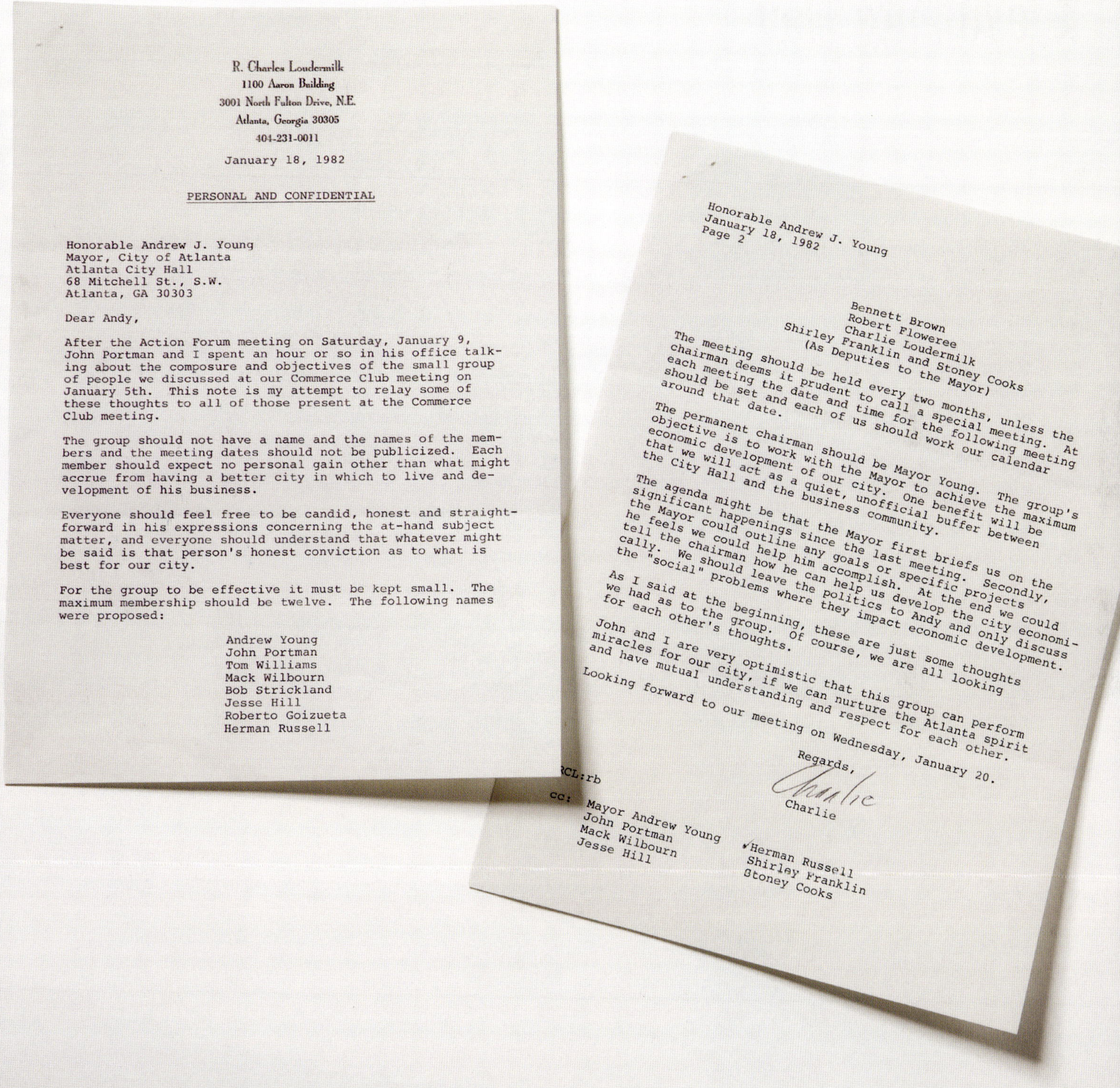

R. Charles Loudermilk
1100 Aaron Building
3001 North Fulton Drive, N.E.
Atlanta, Georgia 30305
404-231-0011

January 18, 1982

PERSONAL AND CONFIDENTIAL

Honorable Andrew J. Young
Mayor, City of Atlanta
Atlanta City Hall
68 Mitchell St., S.W.
Atlanta, GA 30303

Dear Andy,

After the Action Forum meeting on Saturday, January 9, John Portman and I spent an hour or so in his office talking about the composure and objectives of the small group of people we discussed at our Commerce Club meeting on January 5th. This note is my attempt to relay some of these thoughts to all of those present at the Commerce Club meeting.

The group should not have a name and the names of the members and the meeting dates should not be publicized. Each member should expect no personal gain other than what might accrue from having a better city in which to live and development of his business.

Everyone should feel free to be candid, honest and straightforward in his expressions concerning the at-hand subject matter, and everyone should understand that whatever might be said is that person's honest conviction as to what is best for our city.

For the group to be effective it must be kept small. The maximum membership should be twelve. The following names were proposed:

Andrew Young
John Portman
Tom Williams
Mack Wilbourn
Bob Strickland
Jesse Hill
Roberto Goizueta
Herman Russell

Honorable Andrew J. Young
January 18, 1982
Page 2

Bennett Brown
Robert Floweree
Charlie Loudermilk
Shirley Franklin and Stoney Cooks
(As Deputies to the Mayor)

The meeting should be held every two months, unless the chairman deems it prudent to call a special meeting. At each meeting the date and time for the following meeting should be set and each of us should work our calendar around that date.

The permanent chairman should be Mayor Young. The group's objective is to work with the Mayor to achieve the maximum economic development of our city. One benefit will be that we will act as a quiet, unofficial buffer between the City Hall and the business community.

The agenda might be that the Mayor first briefs us on the significant happenings since the last meeting. Secondly, the Mayor could outline any goals or specific projects he feels we could help him accomplish. At the end we could tell the chairman how he can help us develop the city economically. We should leave the politics to Andy and only discuss the "social" problems where they impact economic development.

As I said at the beginning, these are just some thoughts we had as to the group. Of course, we are all looking for each other's thoughts.

John and I are very optimistic that this group can perform miracles for our city, if we can nurture the Atlanta spirit and have mutual understanding and respect for each other.

Looking forward to our meeting on Wednesday, January 20.

Regards,

Charlie

Charlie

RCL:rb

cc: Mayor Andrew Young
John Portman
Mack Wilbourn
Jesse Hill
Herman Russell
Shirley Franklin
Stoney Cooks

Hanson Six

Atlanta's first drivers were licensed in 1904 and by 1916 there were more than 6,000 registered automobiles moving along Atlanta's largely unpaved streets. In the 1920s, Atlanta became a stop on the Dixie Highway (along today's US 41) from Michigan to Florida, a precursor to Interstate 75.

Looking to take part in the auto industry, Georgia native George W. Hanson sold cars in Atlanta for the Studebaker and Saxon companies. In 1916, he founded Hanson Motor Company, joining five other Atlanta manufacturers established between 1909 and 1919: White Star Automobile Company, Southern Motor Car & Truck Company, Primo Motor Company, Southern Auto & Equipment Company, and White Hickory Motor Corporation, each of which closed within a few years.

Hanson Motor Company's first two cars were built from Hanson's designs and the first of these products—the Hanson Six—was introduced at the Southeastern Automobile Show in 1917. The company targeted Southern buyers with slogans, such as "Made in Dixie" and "Tested and Proved in the South," and aimed to build small, light, and moderately priced cars. Hanson's logo was a cotton boll with the words, "Hanson/Atlanta/Ga."

Assembly began at Hanson's southwest Atlanta factory in 1918. By 1919, the Atlanta *City Builder* remarked, "Customers and dealers throughout the country are begging for Hanson Sixes in large numbers," and one business "from a nearby Southern State [requested] the entire output of the factory."

Despite early success, the company produced only 850 vehicles as it suffered from shortages in labor, parts, and materials. Faced with competition from Ford's Atlanta assembly plant and the post–World War I economic downturn, Hanson Motor Company closed in 1925. This Hanson Six is one of two Hanson cars still in existence.

Hanson Six Touring Car
Hanson Motor Company, Atlanta, 1920
Purchase with funds for Metropolitan Frontiers: Atlanta, 1835–2000, 1993

HANSON

Stoneware Jar

On farms across 19th-century Georgia, utilitarian stoneware jars could add a touch of beauty to a rural home. On this example, the simple flowers and drapes of looping script reflect the skilled hand of Thomas Chandler, a potter based near Edgefield, South Carolina.

A migrant from Baltimore, Maryland, Chandler brought the skills of Mid-Atlantic potters to the Southeast backcountry. In the late 1830s, he settled in an area with established potters and a growing number of potential customers as lands newly opened for settlement became farms. Nearby Augusta, Georgia, a transportation center, expanded the market reach of the Edgefield potters.

In distinctive, fluid lines, Chandler created loops, tassels, and other designs on stoneware needed for farm tasks. On buttermilk pitchers and whiskey jugs, Chandler added patterns of flowers or leafy sprigs. A high-luster glaze was applied inside and out, and Chandler then used a watery mixture of clay, known as "slip," colored white with kaolin or brown with iron. With the slip, Chandler added decorative elements to water coolers, milk pans, and four-handled storage vessels. Careful firing at the kiln's high temperatures finished the process.

Chandler's pottery skills included identifying quality local clay for fine stoneware, and he worked as the principal turner at Edgefield's Phoenix Factory. Later, he operated his own Trapp & Chandler pottery factory. The Edgefield pottery tradition was influential, and its practice moved westward to Georgia, Alabama, Mississippi, Louisiana, and Texas. Though the objects they made had a practical use, Chandler—known today as the most skillful potter to work in Edgefield—and his fellow potters created works of lasting beauty.

Food Storage Jar
Thomas Chandler, potter, Trapp & Chandler pottery, Kirksey, South Carolina, circa 1850
Gift of A. Hayes Gilliam, 1984

Decorative Terracotta Panel

For decades, this panel adorned the Norris Candy Company building, the colorful terracotta flowers reminding Atlantans of the delicious treats made inside. Designed by the architectural firm of Pringle & Smith, the eight-story building at 223 Peachtree Street was completed in 1926. Though it was home to other businesses, the building is best known for housing the manufacturing facilities of Norris's line of Exquisite Candies, which ranged from candy making to producing colorful packaging, including eye-catching boxes decorated with images of peach blossoms, floral bouquets, ribbons and bows, or charming children.

The *Atlanta Journal* profiled the layout of the business in 1951. On one floor, machine-dipped chocolates traveled along a 450-foot conveyor belt, while on another a mechanized "candy puller" wound long streams of a melted sugar mixture, transforming the soft, sweet blend into hard candy. On the first floor, the shipping department sent the filled boxes nationwide.

In addition to chocolates, Norris Candy created "Della Robbia Mints." A customer favorite, the mints were inspired by a Norris family trip to Italy, home of Della Robbia sculpture, which features brightly colored, glazed terracotta, often decorated with fruit and flowers.

Architects Pringle & Smith designed five landmark buildings that defined the Atlanta skyline in the early 20th century. Francis Palmer Smith not only designed Atlanta churches, commercial buildings, and residences, but he also trained architects at the recently established Department of Architecture at the Georgia Institute of Technology. He served as director beginning in 1908. The program graduated a number of students that became Atlanta's premier architects, including Philip Trammell Shutze, architect of Atlanta History Center's Swan House.

Terracotta Panel
Pringle & Smith, architects, 1926
Gift of Harold T. Hudgins, 1974

Gillian Head
ORIGINAL
ATLANTA

Lillian Head Hat

In the summer of 1964, the Chandler family prepared for the marriage of their daughter, expecting extra scrutiny since the wedding was one of the first of a Black couple to take place in a historically white church in Atlanta. The bride's mother, Erdie Chandler, wore this hat created by noted Black Atlanta milliner Lillian Head.

During the early 1960s, churches were among the most racially divided spaces in the South. The couple, Beth Chandler and the Rev. John J. Warren, celebrated their wedding at the Episcopal Cathedral of St. Philip with a mix of Black and white bridesmaids and groomsmen. The bride's parents were community leaders. Her father, Dr. Gladstone Chandler, taught at Morehouse College, where civil rights activists were among his students.

In selecting a hat by Lillian Head, Mrs. Chandler was supporting a Black Atlantan who succeeded despite discrimination. As a young woman, Head had been told "white girls do that" when a local Atlanta retail store refused to hire her as a designer. Instead, Head accepted a position as a maid for Loretta Bonta's chic 15th Street atelier.

In that role, she was able to demonstrate her skills and was hired as a designer. Mary McLeod Bethune, one of the nation's most important Black educators and civil and women's rights advocates, invited Head to design a show aimed at integrating the fashion industry.

Head's designs appeared in department stores in New York City alongside the work of her white counterparts. During her career she participated in New York fashion shows, created hats for special occasions, and designed one-of-a-kind pieces for prominent Atlanta women—both Black and white.

Lady's Hat
Lillian B. Head, designer,
Atlanta, 1964
Gift of Erdie Wade Chandler, 1980

Shillinglaw Cookbook Collection

Southern dinner tables reflect culinary influences from around the world. The Shillinglaw Cookbook Collection illustrates changes to Southern tables and communities of cooks with publications from the 17th century to today.

The evolution of one Southern tradition—barbecue—is an example of the history documented by the collection. European explorers encountered Indigenous culinary traditions in North America where the Taíno people used smoke to cook meat on wooden grills called a *barbacot*. The Spanish called this cooking technique *barbacoa*, while the French called it *boucan*. The term was first used in English in the 1707 book *The Barbacue Feast*. As it evolved in North America, barbecue also picked up the flavors of spice blends brought to the colonies by enslaved West Africans. Eventually, this culinary blend became Southern barbecue.

Two centuries later, cookbooks record changes as Southerners adapted to new technology and increased mobility in the 20th century. At the turn of the century, women long accustomed to wood stoves gathered in cooking classes to learn how to use a gas stove from Henrietta Dull, a columnist for the *Atlanta Journal*. Dull, author of the book *Southern Cooking*, became the trusted authority for such Southern classics as turnip greens.

The Shillinglaw Cookbook Collection, which includes more than 600 volumes, was compiled by Dr. Clifford A. Shillinglaw, senior vice president of Coca-Cola Company. In the early 1970s, Shillinglaw became concerned about the possible disappearance of Southern food heritage and created a collection of culinary texts related to its development and preservation. The collection contains a variety of historic and contemporary texts spanning three centuries and continues to expand to encompass the evolving cuisine of the South.

Shillinglaw Cookbook Collection
Dr. Clifford Shillinglaw, 1970s
Gift of Coca-Cola Company, 1979

The Barbacue Feast: Or, The Three Pigs of Peckham, Broil'd under an Apple-Tree . . .
Ned [Edward] Ward
London: Printed and sold by B. Bragge at the Raven in Pater-Noster-Row, 1707
Purchase with funds from Sheffield-Harrold Charitable Trust

Housekeeping and Dinner-Giving in Kansas City
Stove Pilot
FAVORITE RECIPES FROM MAXWELL
Southern Cooking
Mrs S.R. DULL
INTRODUCTION
TO THE FIRST EDITION
FAVORITE PERSONAL RECIPES.
BREAD, BISCUIT, MUFFINS, WAFFLES, ETC.
PAN-AMERICAN RICE BISCUITS.
ABERNETHY BISCUITS.
ARROWROOT BISCUITS.
CHOCOLATE BISCUIT.
THE
BARBACUE FEAST:
OR, THE
Three Pigs of Peckham,
Broil'd under an Apple-Tree:
WHERE
The Cooks were Numberlefs;
The Company Mafterlefs;
The Meat Carv'd with Hatchets;
And Punch drank by Pail-fulls.
By the Author of The Trip to Jamaica.
LONDON,
Printed: And fold by B. Bragge, at the Raven in Pater-Nofter-Row. 1707. Price 6 d.

POW Trousers and Cup

POWs were suddenly thrust into a horrible situation, but through teamwork, love, and support in-prison and abroad, we did our duty with honor and dignity. If that example is our legacy, then we're proud to offer it to the world.

Chaplain Colonel Robert G. Certain, USAF Retired

The U.S. Air Force deployed Robert G. Certain to Vietnam 10 days after he graduated from Emory University. In late 1972, he was captured and placed in the infamous Hỏa Lò Prison, known as the Hanoi Hilton. Notorious for its inhumane treatment of prisoners of war (POWs) and squalid conditions, Certain survived 101 days of captivity.

The POWs shared meager daily rations of cabbage soup, one-half loaf of French bread, and a mug of weak tea or powdered milk. In the bitter winter weather, their striped prison clothes or "clown suit" offered little protection. To keep warm, the men slept close to one another with the most ill men in the center.

More than 200,000 Georgians served in the Vietnam War; 1,581 lost their lives. Returning soldiers were welcomed home by their families and other supporters but faced the reality of a nation that sought to move on from an increasingly unpopular war that most saw as a defeat.

Back in the U.S., Certain was one of many soldiers who internalized their ordeal. He learned to recognize events that triggered traumatic responses and used that knowledge for spiritual and psychological growth. He became an Episcopal priest and dedicated his life to helping others navigate trauma and learn to grow from it.

POW Trousers and Cup
Democratic Republic of Vietnam [North Vietnam], 1972
Gift of Robert Certain, 2016

Jimmy Carter Campaign Button

In 1970, Jimmy Carter paid a visit to the Rev. Martin Luther King Sr. at Ebenezer Baptist Church, a first for a white gubernatorial candidate. As governor, Carter operated differently than previous Georgia officeholders, boldly declaring, "The time for racial discrimination is over." He showed personal and political growth from his background in the Jim Crow South.

By 1975, Carter was exploring a run for president of the United States—a massive leap from his position as the former governor of a state that many in the U.S. did not think about at all or, worse, thought of as slightly backwards. For Jimmy Carter to have a chance of winning the presidency, Black voter support was crucial.

Martin Luther King Sr. agreed to campaign for Carter, seeing potential in the man who shared his rural roots and whom he saw as making concrete advancements in racial equality during his time as governor. Other leaders in the Black community supported Carter as well, including Andrew Young, Atlanta's congressman and Carter's future ambassador to the United Nations. Enthusiastic Georgia citizens—Black and white—also campaigned for Carter as members of the industrious Peanut Brigade, which saw them traveling across the country to canvas for the Georgian.

On election night of 1976, Carter won the contest against incumbent Gerald Ford, becoming the first president from Georgia. The victory was a testament to the efforts of well-known community leaders, campaign experts, and ordinary citizens alike to raise the country's awareness of Carter—efforts in which Atlantans played a crucial role.

Campaign Button

Jimmy Carter Presidential Campaign Committee, Atlanta, 1976

Gift of Leslie Ferst, 2010

Zero Milepost

In 1836, the Georgia General Assembly voted to create the Western & Atlantic Railroad (W&A) to connect a site near the Chattahoochee River to a point close to Georgia's northern state line on the Tennessee River. The southern terminal point, originally called simply Terminus, later grew into the city of Atlanta. Legislation in Tennessee established the northern point of the railroad at Ross's Landing, Tennessee (now Chattanooga).

The southern terminus was relocated a number of times within a half-mile distance until 1842, when Samuel Mitchell donated land for what became State Square. This became the site of two passenger depots: the Union Station of 1853 and Union Station of 1871.

In the 1850s, the W&A placed mileposts along the entire route of the railroad to Chattanooga and placed this one to mark the beginning spot of the railroad in Atlanta. The post is marked "W&A 00" to indicate the beginning of the rail line and, conversely, "W&A 138" to mark the 138th mile from the northern terminal point to Atlanta.

Through the destruction of the first Union Station during the Civil War, the construction of the second Union Station, and the later demolition of that station, this stone milepost remained in its original location. The milepost is now on display at Atlanta History Center, preserved and interpreted in historical context, while a replica marks the original site.

Zero Milepost
Western & Atlantic Railroad, Atlanta, circa 1850
Courtesy Georgia Building Authority, State of Georgia, 2018

Barbecue Rib Shack Sign

When Allen James "A.J." Taylor and his wife Mary opened their restaurant on Auburn Avenue in 1963, they were continuing a long tradition. American barbecue, a cooking technique that involves the slow roasting of meat, developed early in the nation's history.

It was a fusion of culinary traditions from Indigenous North American tribes, enslaved West African peoples, and European colonists. Barbecue was embraced by enslaved Africans and later by poor Black communities to add flavor to inferior meats like ribs. Through their recipes, A.J. and Mary celebrated their heritage and their Sweet Auburn neighborhood.

When A.J. and Mary's restaurant, the Auburn Avenue Rib Shack, opened, it fed many civil rights activists from the organizations headquartered in the Auburn Avenue area. However, the construction and subsequent expansion of a new interstate highway through the neighborhood had a devastating impact on the street's businesses and the restaurant. The highway cut through the heart of the community, leaving businesses disconnected and struggling. The rib shack lasted for more than 30 years and closed in 1995.

Neon Restaurant Sign
Unidentified maker, 1963
Given in honor of Mary and Allen James Taylor by their daughter Dorothy Clements, 1994

The Souls of Black Folk

In 1903, scholar, activist, and Atlanta resident W.E.B. Du Bois published *The Souls of Black Folk*, a collection of essays about Black life in America. After becoming the first Black man to earn a Ph.D. from Harvard University, he was recruited by Atlanta University (now, Clark Atlanta University) to establish its sociology department. Over his 23 years in Atlanta, Du Bois wrote multiple books and established a notable series of conferences and reports on Black social conditions, called the Atlanta University Studies.

In *The Souls of Black Folk*, Du Bois challenged the approach of Booker T. Washington, the most prominent national Black leader of the time. Washington argued that discrimination would "wither away" gradually and that Black Americans should prioritize economic gains and vocational education over pursuing racial integration.

Du Bois argued that accommodation would limit Black citizens to indefinite subservience and that change would require protest. He described in the book the concept of "double-consciousness," the idea that Black individuals feel the need to see themselves both through their own eyes as well as through those of a white supremacist society:

> One ever feels his twoness—an American, a Negro; two souls, two thoughts, two unreconciled strivings; two warring ideals in one dark body, whose dogged strength alone keeps it from being torn asunder.... He simply wishes to make it possible for a man to be both a Negro and an American, without being cursed and spit upon by his fellows, without having the doors of Opportunity closed roughly in his face.

The Souls of Black Folk
Chicago: A.C. McClurg & Company, 1903
Gift of the Estate of Lucy Rucker Aiken, 1992

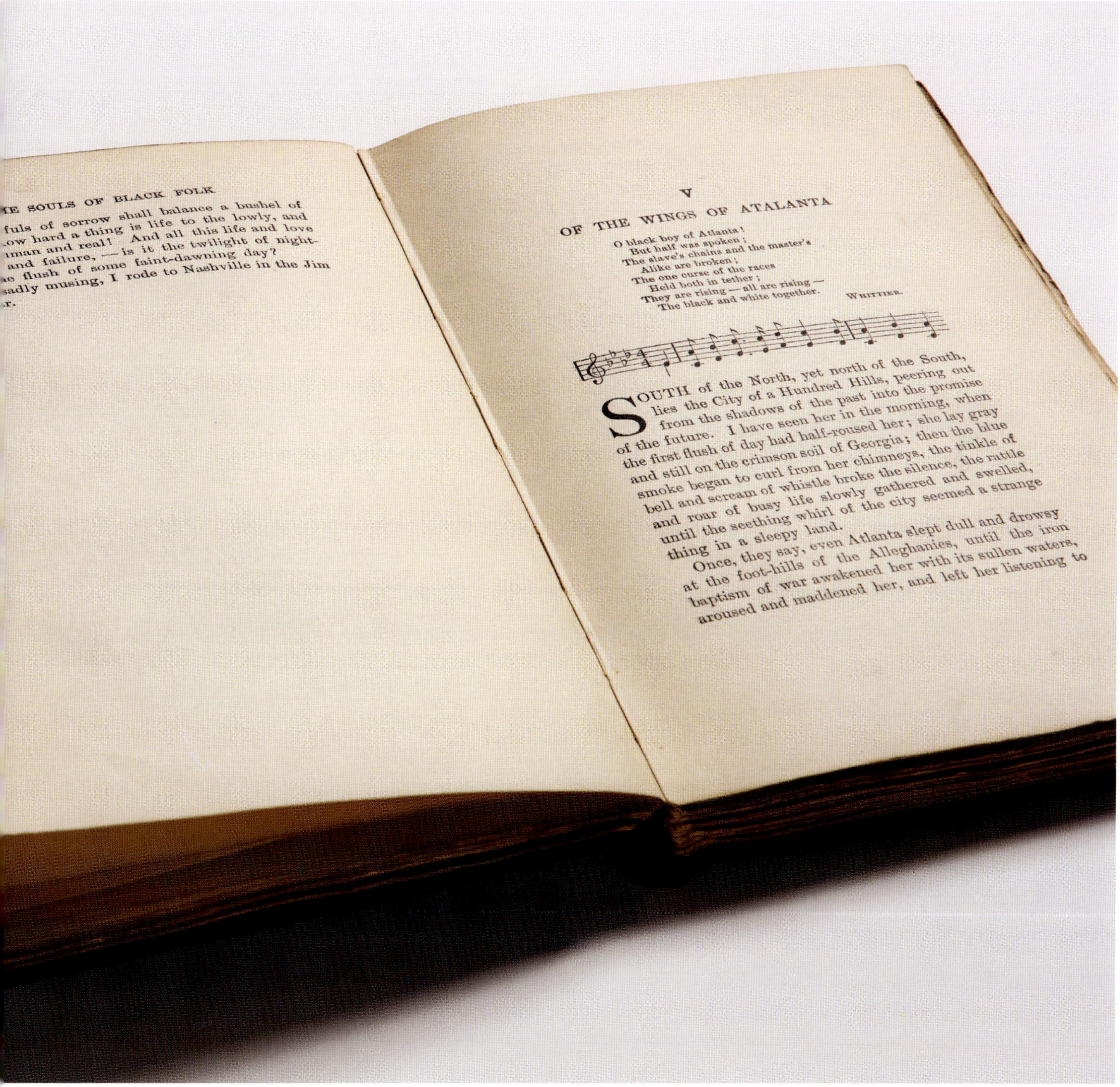
E SOULS OF BLACK FOLK

fuls of sorrow shall balance a bushel of
ow hard a thing is life to the lowly, and
man and real! And all this life and love
and failure, — is it the twilight of night-
e flush of some faint-dawning day?
sadly musing, I rode to Nashville in the Jim
r.

V

OF THE WINGS OF ATALANTA

O black boy of Atlanta!
But half was spoken;
The slave's chains and the master's
Alike are broken;
The one curse of the races
Held both in tether;
They are rising — all are rising —
The black and white together.
WHITTIER.

SOUTH of the North, yet north of the South, lies the City of a Hundred Hills, peering out from the shadows of the past into the promise of the future. I have seen her in the morning, when the first flush of day had half-roused her; she lay gray and still on the crimson soil of Georgia; then the blue smoke began to curl from her chimneys, the tinkle of bell and scream of whistle broke the silence, the rattle and roar of busy life slowly gathered and swelled, until the seething whirl of the city seemed a strange thing in a sleepy land.

Once, they say, even Atlanta slept dull and drowsy at the foot-hills of the Alleghanies, until the iron baptism of war awakened her with its sullen waters, aroused and maddened her, and left her listening to

Death Masks

America's relationship with death and bereavement at the turn of the 19th century relied heavily on public rituals. Cemeteries were designed as parks so families could spend time with the departed. Items of jewelry, such as lockets, were decorated with images of loved ones and often contained a lock of their hair. Death masks were a part of this tradition of simultaneously celebrating life while embracing death.

New York–born artist Orion Frazee made a number of masks during his nine years in Atlanta. These masks could then be used to produce busts and other artwork for families and institutions. Frazee's masks of Henry W. Grady, Lemuel P. Grant, and Richard Peters are part of a collection of Atlanta city leaders.

Henry W. Grady was a friend of Frazee and a subject after his death in 1889. Grady used his position as editor and part owner of the Atlanta Constitution to promote the city as a sound business opportunity for eager Northern investors, adopting the phrase "New South" to encourage Southern modernization after the Civil War.

A railroad engineer, L.P. Grant was a chief engineer in the Confederate Army and designed the fortifications for Atlanta, intended to protect the city against the Union Army of Major General William T. Sherman. Today, Grant is remembered as the namesake for the Grant Park neighborhood and for donating 100 acres that became the city park that bears his name.

Richard Peters made his first visit to the city in 1844 when its name was Marthasville. As superintendent of the Georgia Railroad—he rode in the company's first train to arrive in the city—he was later instrumental in changing the name of the community to Atlanta, bringing the state capital to the city, and creating the Georgia Institute of Technology.

Death Masks
Orion Frazee, artist, Atlanta, 1889–1893
Purchase with funds for the Collections, 2013

Face Jug

Lanier Meaders spent his career looking to the past, creating pottery using the traditional forms and techniques of his community in Mossy Creek, Georgia.

In the early 19th century, when Georgia was largely rural, families turned to local potters for utilitarian vessels for preparing, transporting, and preserving food. Potters found quality clay in the beds of Mossy Creek, located just below the foothills of the Appalachian Mountains. By the 1840s, they had begun a pottery-making tradition. Throughout Georgia, communities of potters like Mossy Creek, sometimes called "jug towns," developed where potters readily found local materials.

As glass and metal containers became widely available in the 20th century, many potters left the trade. The Meaders family, however, continued to make stoneware for collectors and tourists who traveled to Mossy Creek on a newly paved road. Through the end of the 20th century, Lanier Meaders made pottery in the workshop built by his grandfather in 1892.

Southeastern potters, including many enslaved craftspeople, have made face jugs since the mid-1800s, creating a range of styles. In this jug, Meaders used balled kaolin, a white clay available in Georgia, to make the eyes and teeth. Typical of Mossy Creek pots is the dark green glaze, the color created by the presence of iron. Meaders, considered a master craftsman and the most famous 20th-century maker of face jugs, died in 1998 in Mossy Creek, the town where he was born and worked his entire life.

Face Jug
Lanier Meaders, potter, Meaders Pottery, Mossy Creek, Georgia, 1982
Gift of Glen and John E. LaRowe, 1995

P. 39
COCCOTHRAUSTES CÆRULEA.
Gros-Bec bleu.
The Blue Grofs-beak.
Magnolia Lauri folio, fubtus albicant
THE SWEET FLOWRING BAY.

Mark Catesby

These two rare and valuable volumes, published in the 18th century, brought the wonders of the New World to curious Europeans. They contain images of flora and fauna unknown to the scientists and collectors of Europe of the day.

English naturalist Mark Catesby first encountered the flora and fauna of North America during a trip, beginning in 1712, to the colony of Virginia and to the West Indies. With financial backing of sponsors, he crossed the Atlantic again in 1722, this time to the "Province of Carolina," which included modern-day Georgia, North Carolina, South Carolina, parts of Florida, and lands extending to the west.

Providing drawings and specimens of plants and animals to his investors required him to spend months in the field. Catesby explored the southeastern frontier from the coastal plain, up the Savannah River, and into the Piedmont near the Appalachian Mountains. Everywhere he went, Catesby observed and painted unknown wonders of every size: massive buffalo, swallowtail butterflies, bald eagles, flowering laurel, and broadleaf magnolia.

Returning to England, Catesby worked for 20 years to produce a published record of what he saw in North America. In so doing, he created the first fully illustrated study of the natural history of the region. Engravings published in 11 sections contained a total of 220 hand-colored images.

Catesby created a vivid record of the natural riches of the Southeast including bird life now extinct: the Carolina Parakeet and the Passenger Pigeon. Catesby is remembered today as the region's most important plant collector of the colonial era and the first to record the detailed beauty of North American birdlife.

The Natural History of Carolina, Florida, and the Bahama Islands

Mark Catesby, artist and author

London: Printed for C. Marsh, T. Wilcox, and B. Stichall, Volumes 1 and 2, 1754, second edition

Purchase with funds from the Generous Sponsors and Patrons of the Cherokee Garden Library's 50 Years & Growing event, 2025

Kimball Opera House Clock

In January 1869, Atlanta opened the doors of the new state capitol, recently converted from an opera house. While a band played, Atlanta residents strolled through the large rooms, enjoying what the *Atlanta Constitution* called "beyond controversy the finest [building] in the State of Georgia."

The E. Howard & Company clock, with its elegant mahogany case and marble face, adorned the original building. Yet the excitement of the evening was not limited to the building's decorations. The event also celebrated Atlanta's new role as Georgia's state capital.

In 1868, during the post–Civil War state constitutional convention, delegates debated where the capital should be located. Milledgeville, which had been Georgia's capital since 1804, had recently renovated state government buildings and offered more hotel rooms for legislators. Meanwhile, Atlanta, which was campaigning to replace Milledgeville, offered rail access and a cooler climate. When votes were counted, Atlanta, flush with new businesses and growth, was temporarily declared the new capital. In 1877, the move was made permanent.

In preparation for the arrival of Georgia's General Assembly, Atlanta's 1854 city hall was hastily refreshed, but this ultimately proved insufficient. As a result, local businessman Hannibal Kimball offered his services. He oversaw the renovation of his opera house into the state capitol. On completion, he initially rented it to the state for $6,000 per year. The state bought the building in 1870 and remained there for nearly 20 years.

Building Clock
E. Howard & Company, Boston, circa 1869
Gift of Mr. and Mrs. Hugh Howell, 1949

S F
REGULATOR.

Atlanta Crackers

In 1907, the minor league baseball team, the Atlanta Crackers, secured a new playing field about two miles from downtown Atlanta. It was located on a trolley line and across from the Ponce de Leon Springs amusement park. The team's owner, Georgia Railway & Electric Company, filled in the park's lake to create the new ballpark.

A magnolia tree was left standing deep in center field, making it the only ballpark of its size with a tree in the field of play. It became the goal of batters to send the ball into the tree, allowing them to circle the bases before it could be retrieved. Two players succeeded in reaching the 462-foot target: Babe Ruth and Eddie Mathews.

The Crackers had an exceptional record, winning 17 minor league championships, more than any other Southern Association team. They twice won the league's "Grand Slam," comprising the league title; the playoff series; and the association's championship, the Dixie Series. After World War II, attendance soared, drawing more than 400,000 attendees per year.

Ponce de Leon Park also hosted the Atlanta Black Crackers of the Negro Leagues. Dressed in discarded uniforms of the white Crackers, the Black Crackers' games were held on Morehouse College or Morris Brown College campuses when the ballpark was unavailable. In 1938, the Black Crackers won 19 straight games on the way to winning the League's second-half championship.

The popularity of both the white and Black Crackers assured Major League Baseball that Atlantans would be enthusiastic fans of the first major league team in the South when the Braves moved to the city in 1966.

Atlanta Crackers Jersey
Coane Athletic Knits and Clothing Company, Philadelphia, circa 1956
Gift of Buck Riddle, 2012

Crackers
23

Map of the State of Georgia

In the early 19th century, Daniel Sturges, surveyor general of Georgia, was tasked with completing a systematic survey of the state. Georgia lagged behind other new states in finalizing its borders. Additionally, a new state map was needed to reflect border changes after new treaties were negotiated with the Muscogee (Creek) people and white settlement increased in the central part of the state. Sturges administered the first four of Georgia's eight land lotteries, so he had a significant influence on the development of land policies and was familiar with the state he would be mapping.

As part of the mapmaking process, he required surveyors to swear an oath to report true accounts of the land surveyed. That was an important component. In the wake of previous fraudulent schemes, including the Yazoo Land Fraud, which resulted in scandal, and the Pine Barrens Land Fraud, in which inaccurate surveys were used to sell significantly more land than existed in eastern Georgia, the state had to present a trustworthy and reliable official map.

The final map was compiled from manuscript copies of county maps submitted over 14 years. It was published in 1818 by Eleazar Early, brother of former Georgia Governor Peter Early and Sturges's brother-in-law. Engraved by Samuel Harrison and printed by John Melish in Philadelphia, the map is considered the first close analysis of the entire state and the foundation of Georgia's cartographic record.

Noted on the map is Rock Mountain (today's Stone Mountain). The Muscogee settlements of Buzzard's Roost, sometimes called Sandtown, and Standing Peachtree are marked along the Chattahoochee River. Standing Peachtree went on to inspire the use of "Peachtree" as a street name in Atlanta.

Map of the State of Georgia

Daniel Sturges, surveyor; Samuel Harrison, engraver
Savannah: Eleazar Early; Philadelphia: John Melish & Samuel Harrison, 1818

Gift of John K. Hooper in memory of Elizabeth Kontz Hooper, 1998

Delta Air Lines

Delta Air Lines began in 1925 as a crop-dusting company in the agriculture industry. Flight was the newest of many captivating technologies in the early 20th century, but the question remained: how to make money from it?

Huff Daland Dusters, Delta's former name, started in Macon, Georgia, and used small aircraft, dusting crops with pesticide to combat the devastating effects of the boll weevil on cotton plants. Soon, the "puffers," as they were called, moved to Monroe, Louisiana. Its aircraft and skilled pilots worked both the southern U.S. and parts of Central and South America.

In 1928, investors, led by Huff Daland's chief entomologist C.E. Woolman, purchased the company's 20 aircraft, which at the time was one of the largest private fleets in the world. Catherine FitzGerald, the first female employee and board member, suggested the name Delta for the area the company served—the Mississippi Delta region.

The newly formed company introduced passenger service in 1929 and expanded operations to Atlanta's Candler Field in June 1930. At the time, Delta anticipated a new airmail route that would make its fledgling passenger operations financially viable. When the contract failed to materialize, Delta ended passenger service. Airmail routes were rebid by the Post Office Department in 1934 and Delta jumped at the chance to compete—and succeeded. Delta returned to Atlanta with airmail service in July 1934 and resumed passenger service to Atlanta that August.

The introduction of the larger Douglas DC-3 airliner meant that airlines were no longer dependent on airmail subsidies. The new planes made air routes profitable with passengers alone. Delta's first DC-3 was named City of Atlanta on its delivery to Delta in 1940. Less than one year later, Delta moved its company headquarters from Louisiana to Atlanta.

***City of Atlanta* DC-3 Model**
Unidentified maker, 1993
Gift of Delta Air Lines, 1993

DELTA AIR LINES
DELTA AIR LINES
AM 24
CITY OF ATLANTA
U. S. MAIL
DELTA

Reverend Ralph David Abernathy Protest Boots

Starting in the 1950s, civil rights activists took to the streets to demand an end to the racial segregation that had been enforced in the South for generations. Marching with them, standing with them, and praying with them, the Rev. Ralph David Abernathy traveled across the South supporting demonstrators.

Abernathy rose to leadership in the Civil Rights Movement as a pastor in Montgomery, Alabama, when locals boycotted the bus system. The effort ended segregation on buses and launched a long partnership between Abernathy and his fellow pastor Martin Luther King Jr.

Following the Montgomery boycott, the Southern Christian Leadership Conference (SCLC) was founded in Atlanta to build on the boycott's success in Alabama. Moving to Atlanta to become leaders of the SCLC, Abernathy and King also served as pastors—Abernathy at West Hunter Street Baptist Church and King at Ebenezer Baptist Church.

Past efforts to end segregation typically worked through the courts, but the new approach prioritized training protestors in nonviolent resistance. At sit-ins, marches, kneel-ins, rallies, and even wade-ins, SCLC leaders highlighted segregation at public spaces, including beaches and lunch counters. When King's death in 1968 left a need for leadership, Abernathy continued the work, leading a march in Washington a few weeks later and serving as president of the SCLC until 1977.

Today, the SCLC continues to work for economic justice, civil rights, and the eradication of racism.

Work Boots
Inscribed inside: RDA
Sears, Roebuck & Company, Chicago, circa 1965
Courtesy of Juanita Jones Abernathy [Mrs. Rev. Ralph David Abernathy Sr.], 1996

Tramp Art Rocker

The carving on this rocking chair demonstrates the woodworking skills of an innovative, unknown craftsman and the geometric patterns of traditional tramp art. Named for its association with itinerant woodworkers in the latter half of the 19th century, tramp art refers to a form of woodworking decorated with small chips and notches, often made with simple tools such as penknives.

Tramp art has roots in European wood-carving traditions. Immigrants to the U.S. in the late 19th and early 20th centuries popularized these traditional woodworking techniques using found materials like cigar boxes. The Tax Act of 1865 changed how cigars were packaged, and the resulting surfeit of boxes sparked the development of tramp art. Cigar boxes were often made of thin planks of valuable wood, like mahogany, making them attractive to woodworkers. Many tramp art pieces were made of layers of this thin wood, carved with small V-shaped notches.

Tramp artists created a wide variety of objects, such as picture frames, decorative boxes, furnishings, and more. The practice appealed to woodworkers regardless of social class, usually men and boys who had been trained in basic whittling skills since childhood. Though the lives of individual artists are rarely documented, tramp art was clearly made by both middle-class farmers and businessmen looking to fill free evenings and those who had fallen on hard times and were living a nomadic life while looking for work.

Rocking Chair
Unidentified maker, circa 1890
Gift of Robert & Katherine Harrell, 2022

Battle of Atlanta Revolver

At 4:00 p.m. on the afternoon of July 22, 1864, U.S. Army Captain Francis DeGress watched in horror as Confederate forces broke through the Union lines east of Atlanta. The 23-year-old soldier was in command of the four 20-pounder rifled cannons of Battery H, 1st Illinois Light Artillery.

With his position about to be overtaken, DeGress ordered his men to disable two of the guns and run for cover. The Confederates called on DeGress to surrender. He answered by firing the other two guns directly into their ranks. At about 4:45 p.m., DeGress and his men joined Union reinforcements in a counterattack and recaptured their guns.

The Union counterattack is the central action of the 1886 Cyclorama painting *The Battle of Atlanta*. The Cyclorama artists depicted a hatless DeGress on horseback defiantly waving a small revolver. For decades, it was believed that the gesture and the revolver were mere dramatic effects.

In 2006, DeGress descendants discovered a small pocket revolver that their great-grandfather carried into battle that day. They also found a letter by Theodore Davis, a witness to the battle and a friend of DeGress, who was also a historical adviser to the Cyclorama artists. The letter revealed that it was Davis who recommended DeGress's dramatic pose with this revolver.

Pocket Revolver
L.W. Pond Machine & Foundry Company, Worcester, Massachusetts, 1863
Gift of the late Peter DeGress and Susan DeGress Maynard, 2008

Blanket Chest

Homes on the Georgia frontier typically included a few pieces of furniture to meet the basic needs of households: a table, chairs, bed, and a storage chest—commonly known as a blanket chest. Before closets became common in American homes, chests stored clothes, blankets, and other items. Farm families were largely self-sufficient, and many Georgians made their own furniture. Their furnishings of the era, often described as "plain style," reflect the needs of farm households for utility and simplicity.

Georgia's frontier population grew rapidly in the early 1800s as Muscogee (Creek) and Cherokee peoples, having lost their lands by cessations and force, were removed and white settlers established small farms on those lands. Farmers with few or no enslaved workers quickly became the largest group of white Southerners in the state, and their small holdings became the most common agricultural unit.

Simple chests stored textiles often made by farm wives who wove cloth, sewed clothes, and made quilts and coverlets that provided warmth on cold nights. Chests often became family heirlooms. Some modern Georgians recall the chest as a place to store precious items, including a family Bible.

This simple chest stands out with its bright green color. Ornamental painting was present in everyday life in early Georgia on signs, walls, and furniture. Advertisements offered various types and colors of paint, which was widely sold throughout the state. Plain-style furniture, painted to enhance its effect on a home, might include a decorative design or a single color, most commonly blue, green, ocher, brown, black, or red.

Blanket Chest
Unidentified maker,
Walker County, Georgia,
circa 1845
Purchase with funds for Tullie Smith House, 1982

An Appeal for Human Rights

In the spring of 1960, students at Atlanta's historically Black colleges published an appeal for the right to share in "long awaited rights and privileges" afforded to white Americans. Inspired by sit-ins at lunch counters in Greensboro, North Carolina, the students planned to organize demonstrations in Atlanta. They formed the Committee on the Appeal for Human Rights and published their declaration at the urging of local university presidents. In it, the students attempted to explain their reasons for protesting.

The resulting essay cited numerous inequalities and injustices in education, housing, voting, health, employment, and law enforcement. The appeal challenged public officials and all "people of goodwill" to live up to Atlanta's progressive reputation. "We want to state clearly and unequivocally," they wrote, "that we cannot tolerate, in a nation professing democracy and among people professing Christianity, the discriminatory conditions under which the Negro is living today."

The students concluded: "We must say in all candor that we plan to use every legal and non-violent means at our disposal to secure full citizenship rights as members of this great Democracy of ours."

Six days after publishing the appeal in three Atlanta newspapers, the group began organized sit-ins at segregated Atlanta lunch counters. In the coming years, the students led efforts to desegregate public spaces in Atlanta and across Georgia. The members of what became known as the Atlanta Student Movement advanced the goal of social equality and helped position Atlanta as the cradle of the Civil Rights Movement.

An Appeal for Human Rights
Atlanta: Unidentified printer, 1960
Gift of Metropolitan Atlanta Rapid Transit Authority (MARTA), 1977

AN APPEAL FOR HUMAN RIGHTS

We, the students of the six affiliated institutions forming the Atlanta University Center — Clark, Morehouse, Morris Brown, and Spelman Colleges, Atlanta University, and the Interdenominational Theological Center—have joined our hearts, minds, and bodies in the cause of gaining those rights which are inherently ours as members of the human race and as citizens of these United States.

We pledge our unqualified support to those students in this nation who have recently been engaged in the significant movement to secure certain long-awaited rights and privileges. This protest, like the bus boycott in Montgomery, has shocked many people throughout the world. Why? Because they had not quite realized the unanimity of spirit and purpose which motivates the thinking and action of the great majority of the Negro people. The students who instigate and participate in these sit-down protests are dissatisfied, not only with the existing conditions, but with the snail-like speed at which they are being ameliorated. Every normal human being wants to walk the earth with dignity and abhors any and all proscriptions placed upon him because of race or color. In essence, this is the meaning of the sit-down protests that are sweeping this nation today.

We do not intend to wait placidly for those rights which are already legally and morally ours to be meted out to us one at a time. Today's youth will not sit by submissively, while being denied all of the rights, privileges, and joys of life. We want to state clearly and unequivocally that we cannot tolerate, in a nation professing democracy and among people professing Christianity, the discriminatory conditions under which the Negro is living today in Atlanta, Georgia—supposedly one of the most progressive cities in the South.

Among the inequalities and injustices in Atlanta and in Georgia against which we protest, the following are outstanding examples:

(1) Education:

In the Public School System, facilities for Negroes and whites are separate and unequal. Double sessions continue in about half of the Negro Public Schools, and many Negro children travel ten miles a day in order to reach a school that will admit them.

On the university level, the state will pay a Negro to attend a school out of state rather than admit him to the University of Georgia, Georgia Tech, the Georgia Medical School, and other tax-supported public institutions.

According to a recent publication, in the fiscal year 1958 a total of $31,632,057.18 was spent in the State institutions of higher education for white only. In the Negro State Colleges only $2,001,177.06 was spent.

The publicly supported institutions of higher education are inter-racial now, except that they deny admission to Negro Americans.

(2) Jobs:

Negroes are denied employment in the majority of city, state, and federal governmental jobs, except in the most menial capacities.

(3) Housing:

While Negroes constitute 32% of the population of Atlanta, they are forced to live within 16% of the area of the city.

Statistics also show that the bulk of the Negro population is still:

a. locked into the more undesirable and overcrowded areas of the city;

b. paying a proportionally higher percentage of income for rental and purchase of generally lower quality property;

c. blocked by political and direct or indirect racial restrictions in its efforts to secure better housing.

(4) Voting:

Contrary to statements made in Congress recently by several Southern Senators, we know that in many counties in Georgia and other southern states, Negro college graduates are declared unqualified to vote and are not permitted to register.

(5) Hospitals:

Compared with facilities for other people in Atlanta and Georgia, those for Negroes are unequal and totally inadequate.

Reports show that Atlanta's 14 general hospitals and 9 related institutions provide some 4,000 beds. Except for some 430 beds at Grady Hospital, Negroes are limited to the 250 beds in three private Negro hospitals. Some of the hospitals barring Negroes were built with federal funds.

(6) Movies, Concerts, Restaurants:

Negroes are barred from most downtown movies and segregated in the rest.

Negroes must even sit in a segregated section of the Municipal Auditorium.

If a Negro is hungry, his hunger must wait until he comes to a "colored" restaurant, and even his thirst must await its quenching at a "colored" water fountain.

(7) Law Enforcement:

There are grave inequalities in the area of law enforcement. Too often, Negroes are maltreated by officers of the law. An insufficient number of Negroes is employed in the law-enforcing agencies. They are seldom, if ever promoted. Of 830 policemen in Atlanta only 35 are Negroes.

We have briefly mentioned only a few situations in which we are discriminated against. We have understated rather than overstated the problems. These social evils are seriously plaguing Georgia, the South, the nation, and the world.

We hold that:

(1) The practice of racial segregation is not in keeping with the ideals of Democracy and Christianity.

(2) Racial segregation is robbing not only the segregated but the segregator of his human dignity. Furthermore, the propagation of racial prejudice is unfair to the generations yet unborn.

(3) In times of war, the Negro has fought and died for his country; yet he still has not been accorded first-class citizenship.

(4) In spite of the fact that the Negro pays his share of taxes, he does not enjoy participation in city, county and state government at the level where laws are enacted.

(5) The social, economic, and political progress of Georgia is retarded by segregation and prejudices.

(6) America is fast losing the respect of other nations by the poor example which she sets in the area of race relations.

It is unfortunate that the Negro is being forced to fight, in any way, for what is due him and is freely accorded other Americans. It is unfortunate that even today some people should hold to the erroneous idea of racial superiority, despite the fact that the world is fast moving toward an integrated humanity.

The time has come for the people of Atlanta and Georgia to take a good look at what is really happening in this country, and to stop believing those who tell us that everything is fine and equal, and that the Negro is happy and satisfied.

It is to be regretted that there are those who still refuse to recognize the over-riding supremacy of the Federal Law.

Our churches which are ordained by God and claim to be the houses of all people, foster segregation of the races to the point of making Sunday the most segregated day of the week.

We, the students of the Atlanta University Center, are driven by past and present events to assert our feelings to the citizens of Atlanta and to the world.

We, therefore, call upon all people in authority—State, County, and City officials; all leaders in civic life—ministers, teachers, and business men; and all people of good will to assert themselves and abolish these injustices. We must say in all candor that we plan to use every legal and non-violent means at our disposal to secure full citizenship rights as members of this great Democracy of ours.

Willie Mays
President of Dormitory Council For the Students of Atlanta University

James Felder
President of Student Government Association For the Students of Clark College

Marion D. Bennett
President of Student Association For the Students of Interdenominational Theological Center

Don Clarke
President of Student Body For the Students of Morehouse College

Mary Ann Smith
Secretary of Student Government Association For the Students of Morris Brown College

Roslyn Pope
President of Student Government Association For the Students of Spelman College

Dallas Austin wuz HERE
"11-17-23"
LOVE IS GOD
GOD IS LOVE
REMEMBER TO CARE FOR YOUR BROTHERS
VOLUME
PROGRAM
COMBINATION
MULTI GLOBAL COMPARE
UTILITY
micro X
SYNTHESIZER / CONTROLLER
KORG

Dallas Austin Synthesizer

Record producer Dallas Austin, born in Columbus, Georgia, set his sights on Atlanta at a young age. After his brother Claude broke his keyboard, the frustrated teenager caught a bus to the city to live with his aunt Clara. His mother, Dianna Austin, known as "Ma Belle," wanting to keep the family together, sold the family restaurant and nightclub, and moved to Atlanta to help Austin follow his musical ambitions.

Atlanta in the 1980s was electric, and the arts and culture scene was undergoing a seismic shift. Graffiti was recognized as art, and the city's developing hip-hop scene was exploding. In 1988, Joyce "Fenderella" Irby, a member of the all-female group Klymaxx, signed the 18-year-old Austin to write and produce music. After years of struggling to get his projects widely distributed, he eventually broke out, producing and writing many of the tracks on *Cooleyhighharmony*, the debut album of the Motown artists Boyz II Men.

In 1992, Atlanta's LaFace Records hired Austin to work with the female R&B group TLC. Austin continued to work with TLC throughout the 1990s and, in 1999, he co-produced TLC's Grammy Award–winning album *Fanmail*. In the 1990s, R&B moved on from its traditional sound to focus on synthesizers, software loops, and samples. Multi-instrumentalist Austin pioneered the new sound and opened his own recording studio.

By the time Austin was inducted into the Songwriters Hall of Fame in 2019, he had more than 50 hit singles. Austin's career reflects Atlanta's international musical influence, which includes a variety of groups, artists, and producers, such as TLC, OutKast, Ludacris, Usher, Lil Jon, Goodie Mob, Killer Mike, Jermaine Dupri, and T.I.

MicroX Synthesizer
Korg, Tokyo, Japan, 2006
Gift of Dallas Austin, 2023

Land Deed: District 17, Land Lot 231

A Muscogee (Creek) settlement and trading center, Pakanahuili, stood at the confluence of the Chattahoochee River and Peachtree Creek. Archaeologists have discovered artifacts there dating as far back as 8000 BCE. The settlement's Muscogee name translates as Standing Peachtree.

Between 1805 and 1833, state-run land lotteries redistributed property formerly inhabited by Muscogee and Cherokee people, including land gained through the First Treaty of Indian Springs of 1821. The lottery following that treaty included the site of present-day Atlanta.

In 1827, the Georgia legislature authorized sale of land that had not been awarded in lotteries, such as fractional surveys, set-asides, and islands in the Chattahoochee River. This included partial Lot 231, comprising only 183 acres (the 1821 land lots were 202.5 acres). The lot to be sold contained the site of Pakanahuili.

Alston Hunter Green purchased the lot in 1833 for $4.50. Green already owned extensive property along the Chattahoochee River southwest of the location of Standing Peachtree. Green Street, later called Hunter Street, was named in his honor; today it is known as Martin Luther King Jr. Drive.

Of all the historic sites in the Atlanta area, Standing Peachtree remains the most iconic. The site inspired multiple street names, all with some variation of Peachtree—or Peach Tree, as it was listed on the original 1821 survey.

State of Georgia Land Deed
Surveyed September 21, 1821; Deed to Alston Hunter Green, March 6, 1833
Gift of Virlyn B. Moore Jr., 1993

MAGNETIC VARIATION
EAST.
STATE OF GEORGIA.
The above Plat is a representation of that Fractional Tract or Lot of Land, purchased by
Alston H Greene
District, Dekalb
County, situate in
the Seventeenth District, in the County of Henry
containing one hundred & eighty three acres
which
is known and distinguished in the plan of said district by the number 231
Surveyed on the 21st day of Sep
1821
By J. Terrell
Surveyor.
Wm McCurley
Micajah Goodwin
C.C.
Lumpkin
Wilson
STATE OF GEORGIA
1799

Kimball House Stained Glass Window

When the Kimball House hotel reopened in 1885 after a fire devastated the original building, newspapers gushed over the lush interiors. The *Chicago Inter Ocean* noted that W.H. Wells & Company of Chicago filled an "extensive stained glass order for the Kimball House," including this window for the dining room.

Ornate stained glass depicting natural subjects was the height of interior design at this time. Raving that the hotel was the "most magnificent in the South," the *Atlanta Journal* detailed the Kimball House's luxuries. Most exciting were the electric lights illuminating the 357 private rooms, 22 public rooms, and 31 business spaces. The building was meant to dazzle, and it succeeded brilliantly.

Hannibal I. Kimball, the man behind the extravagant building, arrived in Atlanta years earlier as a representative of a sleeper-car company from Chicago. Kimball befriended Republican Governor Rufus Bullock and other Atlanta elites. Noticing a lack of hotels and a chance at financial gain, he promptly shifted from railroads to housing the passengers the trains delivered.

Kimball's vision and showmanship were extraordinary, but his fiscal acumen was not. After running over budget in the rebuilding of the hotel, Kimball sold it to local entrepreneur Hugh T. Inman. When Inman's daughter Annie married banker John W. Grant in 1893, her father presented them with the Kimball House as a wedding gift.

Stained Glass Window
W.H. Wells & Company, Chicago, 1885
Gift of Carolyn Becknell Mann, Elizabeth Virginia Alexandra Grace Louise Abbey Mann, and George David William Becknell Mann, 2005

BA

Bagley Park

In the 1940s, more than 50 Black families lived in modest residences in an area of today's Buckhead neighborhood. Formerly enslaved families had settled there in the 1870s when the area was well outside Atlanta's city limits, calling it Macedonia Park. William and Ida Bagley purchased land in the area in 1928 after losing their home in the forced expulsion of Black residents in nearby Forsyth County in 1912. In a testament to William Bagley's leadership in the community, the area became known as Bagley Park.

By 1942, Fulton County officials were receiving complaints from residents in adjacent Garden Hills about their Black neighbors' noise and the lack of a sewage system. Instead of installing sewer lines as it had done in nearby neighborhoods, Fulton County made plans to remove the homes to create a public park. Black-owned homes were purchased or acquired through eminent domain.

The new public park was named Bagley Park until 1980 when city officials renamed it in honor of local baseball umpire Frankie Allen. Descendants of William Bagley saved the historic Bagley Park sign.

In 2022, the park was renamed Historic Bagley Park, honoring William Bagley and the many Black families that had once called Bagley Park home.

Bagley Park Sign
Unidentified maker, circa 1952
Courtesy of Elon Butts Osby, 2023

Leila Ross Wilburn Plan Books

Architect Leila Ross Wilburn transformed the expectation that a woman's place was in the home into a reputation for being the best qualified to *design* a home. With the variety of options in her plan books, which included colonial, bungalow, craftsman, and ranch styles, she designed houses across the Southeast and built a career spanning five decades.

At age 23, Wilburn opened her architectural office in downtown Atlanta, following studies at today's Agnes Scott College and an apprenticeship with Atlanta architectural and construction firm B.R. Padgett & Son to learn drafting skills. Her early projects were single-family homes, though she executed other commissions, including apartment buildings. Wilburn published her first plan book, *Southern Homes and Bungalows*, in 1914, and eight others followed through 1960.

Wilburn's designs targeted the growing middle class, offering small, affordable homes that included details more common to expensive residences. In her 1921 plan book, she told readers, "I feel that, being a woman, I know just the little things that should go in a house to make living in it a pleasure for the entire family."

The early years of Wilburn's practice were well-timed: Atlanta and other cities were growing rapidly. Expanded trolley service and the automobile made life on the city's edge attractive, and her *Small Low-Cost Homes for the South* were well-suited for the new suburbs.

No record exists of the number of homes built from nearly 700 plan book designs, but Atlanta's historic neighborhoods contain examples of Wilburn's architecture as a reminder of her popularity. Thanks to her plan books, towns in seven states across the Southeast also include Wilburn's designs.

Architectural Plan Books
Atlanta: Leila Ross Wilburn, 1920s–1930s
Gift of Susan Hunter, 1982

LEILA ROSS WILBURN, ARCHITECT
IDEAL HOMES OF TODAY
BRICK AND COLONIAL HOMES
RANCH and COLONIAL HOMES
$1.00
Leila Ross Wilburn-Architect
205 One Peachtree (Peters) Building
Atlanta, Georgia

PABST BLUE RIBBON BEER
PURITAN CHEMICAL COMPANY SANITARY SUPPLIES
MAIN 1321 1322
DRINK Schlitz
IT'S PAUSE TIME Coca-Cola DELICIOUS AND REFRESHING
COMPANY
ATLANTA

Parade of Progress

In February 1939, J. Richardson Jones, public relations director for the Atlanta Life Insurance Company, premiered a 30-minute promotional newsreel entitled *Parade of Progress of Colored Atlanta.*

This image from the film features John and Billie Harden. In the 1930s, the couple purchased Atlanta's beloved Black Crackers baseball team. Using the money earned from their Auburn Avenue gas station, the couple bought equipment, uniforms, and even a bus for the team. Morehouse and Morris Brown Colleges supplied many of the players, and the games were often played on their fields to save money.

Atlanta Life Insurance's goal for the film was to "build friendships, and show others what we are doing," and also make money. Relying on his background as a journalist, cinematographer, and actor, Jones delivered a film celebrating a successful, vibrant Black community. The film is filled with images of prosperous businesses, schools, flourishing neighborhoods, and Black Atlantans enjoying leisure activities.

Founded as the Atlanta Benevolent and Protective Association, the business assisted Black individuals and small businesses and accumulated funds with weekly fees. Later, as Atlanta Life Insurance Company, the original principles of community uplift and reinvestment grew under the leadership of entrepreneur Alonzo Herndon, one of the city's first Black millionaires. The company also helped to promote racial solidarity and community interests by providing loans for Black institutions.

Parade of Progress of Colored Atlanta
Joseph Richardson Jones, producer, 1938
Gift of John and Lillian Goodlett, 1994

Atlanta Constitution Desk

For 109 years, this desk was for the editor of the *Atlanta Constitution*. It was originally used by Henry W. Grady, who earned an international reputation for his advocacy for a "New South" focused on industry. It was later used by Joel Chandler Harris, author of the *Uncle Remus* stories.

In the mid-20th century, editor Ralph McGill charmed and challenged his readers in a daily column for more than 30 years. Seated at this desk, McGill wrote columns that asked readers to think in new ways about the vast economic and social changes happening in the region.

McGill's essays often celebrated Southern traditions. He praised the mule, a longtime presence on the Southern farm, and wrote columns about life in small towns. He even accepted a reader's challenge to be the final arbiter on Southern cooking, offering his view on the proper way to make Brunswick stew. In a column written in the years of rapid modernization in the South, McGill devoted a column to his request: "Let's just leave one dirt road."

But McGill also rejected the white South's long conspiracy of silence on discussing racism. A rare voice for change in the mid-century South, McGill earned a Pulitzer Prize in 1959 for his work. He asked white people to let go of their animosity toward their Black neighbors, reminding them, "When the wolves of hate are loosed on one people, no one is safe." Though he angered some people, McGill's words helped reshape the views of many Southerners.

In the mid-1990s, the desk was moved into columnist Celestine Sibley's office. The last journalist to use it was syndicated columnist and editorial page editor Cynthia Tucker.

Roll-top Desk
Unidentified maker, circa 1880
Gift of Atlanta Journal-Constitution, 2009

BILLS
BILLS
BILLS

Flapper Dresses

For women, the 1920s represented a new era and the opportunity for a new look. World War I had ended, and prosperity was on the horizon. The 19th Amendment, granting women the vote, was the law of the land, and women entered the workforce in record numbers. The restrictive clothing of previous generations simply would not do, and the flapper dress accommodated the movement women in the 1920s desired.

Though the origins of the term "flapper" are unknown, its definition is not. It described young women who wore short skirts, bobbed their hair, danced vibrantly, defied prohibition by drinking in speakeasies, and engaged in other behaviors that would have been shocking—or at least startling—to their elders.

Traditional understandings of femininity embraced motherhood and home. In the early 20th century, however, larger paychecks and more leisure time gave women the freedom to explore new things. One example was their clothing. Women of all economic levels adopted the new, simple structure of the flapper style.

While at work, the flapper silhouette deemphasized the figure, and lightweight fabric allowed for freedom of movement. Evening wear was adorned with beads, sequins, and elaborate patterns. Accessories like ornamented purses and headbands, coupled with bold jewelry, completed outfits that could be seen at both speakeasies and opera houses.

1920s Designs

Miscellaneous makers, France and United States, 1920–1925

Gifts of Mrs. Charles Barton, 1982; Edna J. Bowels, 1981; High Museum of Art, 1983; Jack J. Robertson, 1978; and Emmakate Vretman Moore and Emmakate Moore Young in memory of Emmakate Amorous Vretman, 1998

Outwrite Bookstore Sign

When Outwrite Bookstore & Coffeehouse hosted its last author reading in 2012, its doors may have been closing, but its message of inclusivity remained in Atlanta's Midtown neighborhood and beyond.

The LGBTQ+ bookstore and coffee shop was established in 1993 by Philip Rafshoon in Midtown Promenade, a neighborhood shopping center. He sought to fill a void in the city for books on gay and lesbian life, literature, and the arts. An earlier bookshop, Christopher's Kind, established a presence in Atlanta in the early 1980s, but was targeted by police and closed by 1986.

By the time Outwrite moved to a new, larger location on Piedmont Avenue at 10th Street near Piedmont Park in 1996, Atlanta's LGBTQ+ community was growing rapidly. Outwrite filled a gap left by the private homes and bars that characterized LGBTQ+ gathering spots at

the time. It was available to the neighborhood during the day, though it also hosted author events at night.

The bookstore became a destination for community, sharing information, learning about events, celebrating, and sometimes mourning. Outwrite's large glass windows offered a place to connect and to be seen while its interior offered customers a safe environment. Outwrite's public presence challenged notions that queer community gatherings had to be held in restricted and private spaces.

After nearly 20 years, Outwrite closed as online bookstores and social media replaced the demand for physical spaces. Yet the impact of Outwrite can still be felt in Midtown—the vibrant and welcoming neighborhood it called home and helped to create.

Promotional Sign
Jay Frandsen, maker, 1993
Gift of Philip Rafshoon, 2017

Virginia is for lovers.
RALLY
DATE
TIME
CITY
PLACE
get out and vote
September 3rd
GET OUT
AND VOTE
RAZA UNIDA
PARTY

John Lewis

Photojournalist Boyd Lewis came of age in the counterculture of the early 1960s—the "hippie" culture, as he called it. After one photography class at the University of Memphis, he was hooked. At his first job at the *Meridian Star* in Mississippi, however, he made the mistake of contradicting the police and was run out of town.

Lewis eventually found a home at Black-owned newspapers, including *Atlanta Voice* and *Atlanta Inquirer,* where he connected with civil rights activists. Capturing the hippie life and culture of Midtown Atlanta in the 1960s and 1970s, he also documented the Civil Rights Movement. Of his many photographs of the period, his favorites included photographing John Lewis and Julian Bond during their work with the Voter Education Project (VEP).

When John Lewis assumed leadership of VEP in 1970, he was well prepared. His experience with protests in Selma, Alabama, and elsewhere confirmed for him the importance of expanding the vote. Initially focused on enrolling Black voters in the South, the project soon engaged with Native Americans, poor whites, and Mexican Americans through other organizations, such as the Hispanic political group Raza Unida.

John Lewis traveled constantly, often putting in 12-hour days, including a voter registration campaign in Mississippi where he made 37 stops in 25 counties in only one month. During his travels, he heard about intimidation at the polls and the difficulty of overcoming lifelong habits of nonparticipation. In 1975, Lewis lobbied for the renewal of the Voting Rights Act. In August of that year, President Gerald R. Ford signed amendments to the Voting Rights Act of 1965, extending certain provisions of the law to an additional seven years and making some provisions permanent, such as the ban on literacy tests and other barriers to registration and voting.

Voter Education Project Director John Lewis
Boyd Lewis, photographer, Atlanta, 1975
Gift of Boyd Lewis, 1985

Hand-painted Pitcher

By the turn of the 20th century, increased leisure time and wealth created demand for both luxury goods and new pursuits. One such pursuit, particularly popular with women, was painting porcelain.

One common theme was floral decorations, including the poppies chosen by Atlanta resident and skilled artist Irene Smillie. She painted in a stylized fashion that reflected trends of the day. American painters often chose quality blank European porcelain for decorating, and this pitcher was made in Limoges, France.

Painting porcelain was a profession as well as an activity for upper-class women such as Smillie. Decorating porcelain was viewed as an appropriate pursuit for women because it involved creating something for the home. Smillie studied art at the School of Technology in New Jersey after graduating from Washington Seminary, a private school for young ladies of Atlanta. Her art studies set her apart from many other porcelain painters of the time.

A few years after painting this pitcher, Smillie traveled to Europe, continuing her art education. Her 1911 journal records her travels to Rome, Florence, Paris, and London with pages of notes describing the artworks she saw there. World War I interrupted the supply of high-quality European porcelain to the U.S., and hand-painted porcelain largely fell out of favor as styles changed in the postwar years.

Pitcher
Irene Rose Smillie, decorator, 1907
A. Klingenberg & Charles Dwenger, porcelain manufacturer, Limoges, France, circa 1900
Gift of the Estate of Irene Rose Smillie, 1956

Goizueta Gardens

Goizueta Gardens is a 33-acre landscape encompassing a variety of cultivated gardens and preserved woodland, including diverse plant collections and heritage-breed animals.

The gardens celebrate the life of Goizueta Gardens honoree Olga "Olguita" C. de Goizueta.

The ornamental **Olguita's Garden** (below) blooms throughout the year with a tapestry of flowering and foliage plants selected for color, fragrance, texture, and an English garden aesthetic.

Transformed from a 25-foot-deep former rock quarry, the **Mary Howard Gilbert Memorial Quarry Garden** (above) holds Georgia's largest native plant collection in one place. Its plants were once used for medicinal and spiritual purposes by Muscogee (Creek) people and early settlers.

Inspired by the New Perennial Movement and interest in sustainable landscapes, the **Entrance Gardens** (right) feature sweeps of perennials and pollinator-attracting plants with an emphasis on native plants and grasses.

Covered by a high canopy, a brook runs through the **Sims Asian Garden** (left). Satsuki azaleas peak in spring with hydrangeas in summer, followed by Japanese maples providing fall color.

An abundance of springtime azaleas bloom in the **Frank A. Smith Memorial Rhododendron Garden** (right). Evergreens and winter-blooming shrubs begin the year, giving way to azaleas in spring and then blossoms of summer hydrangeas.

Inspired by classical Italian gardens, **Swan House Gardens** (below) is perched on a hill with a cascading fountain, terraced lawns, rose-covered stone walls, and clipped hedges. An intimate boxwood garden and formal entrance court make this one of Atlanta's best-known and most-photographed sites.

With curated gardens and native forest, no other place in Atlanta captures the variety of landscapes that shaped the city's history. In addition to the six gardens illustrated here, **Goizueta Gardens** includes **Smith Farm Gardens**, **Swan Woods**, and **Veterans Park**.

The Battle of Atlanta Cyclorama Painting and Sketch

In the summer of 1885, a dozen artists traveled to Atlanta to create preliminary sketches for *The Battle of Atlanta* Cyclorama, a panoramic painting 371 feet long and almost 50 feet tall. Artists added grid lines on small drawings to reproduce the sketch at the large scale of the final painting. Weeks later, an artist used this sketch, dropping paint on it as he worked on the enormous canvas.

In this sketch, the Troup Hurt house is shown on the late afternoon of July 22, 1864. The house is surrounded by Confederate soldiers fighting to defend their position and the store of artillery captured from federal troops earlier that afternoon.

Today, the Cyclorama painting brings to life a key battle of the Civil War. At Atlanta History Center, the public sees the panoramic painting based on this sketch and the accompanying exhibitions that tell stories of its creation, history, and the public's changing understanding of it. Through the Cyclorama, they can explore the larger question of how our memory and knowledge about the past can be shaped, or mis-shaped, in the convergence of history, art, entertainment, and myth.

***The Battle of Atlanta* Cyclorama Painting and Sketch**
American Panorama Company, Milwaukee, 1885–1886
Painting: *Courtesy City of Atlanta, 2015*
Sketch: *Purchase with funds for the Collection, 2006*

Swan House

The origin of the name Swan House was, as the home's architect Philip Trammell Shutze recalled, "entirely of [its owner] Mrs. Inman's choosing." The name was noted in a 1947 article in the *Atlanta Constitution*, "Names of Atlanta Homes Boast of Unusual Origins." Though the article does not reveal such an origin, "it has been discovered that [Mrs. Inman] calls her place Swan House."

The inspiration for the name may have been the carved and gilded console tables in the dining room. Made in the mid-1700s by English furniture maker Thomas Johnson, each table includes a pair of swans amid golden bulrushes. Emily Inman, an Atlanta suffragist and wife of wealthy businessman Edward Inman, purchased them in Bath, England, in 1924.

Two years later, and seeking a new home in Atlanta's Buckhead neighborhood, the couple hired the firm Hentz, Reid & Adler. One of their young, celebrated architects, Shutze, assumed lead design of the house and gardens. Ruby Ross Wood, a Georgia native working out of New York, was the interior decorator. Wood was at the forefront of the relatively new profession of interior design.

The Inmans moved into the house in 1928. When her husband died suddenly in 1931, at age 49, Mrs. Inman invited her son, Hugh, and his wife, Mildred, to move into the house with their two young children. They remained until the children were grown. In late 1965, Emily died, and Atlanta History Center acquired the property.

The home that Emily Inman, Ruby Ross Wood, and Philip Trammell Shutze created remains a centerpiece of Atlanta History Center, appearing almost exactly as it did in 1928.

Swan Table
Thomas Johnson, Bath, England, circa 1750
Gift of the Forward Arts Foundation, 1974

Swan House
Emily and Edward H. Inman residence, 1928
Philip Trammell Shutze, architect, and Ruby Ross Wood, decorator
Purchase from the Estate of Mrs. Edward H. Inman, 1966

Smith Farm

The Smith family built this farmhouse in about 1845 when DeKalb County was a rural landscape dotted with crossroad communities. Nearby towns included Atlanta, about eight miles away, with more than 2,500 residents. Most people in the area, however, lived in the country, farming cotton and food for their families. The farmhouse represents the lifestyle typical for an upper-middle-class family of the time, and it was designed to maximize ventilation and light. Built in a style once common for farmhouses, it is shallow, just two rooms deep, upstairs and downstairs.

The last resident of the house was Tullie Smith, great-granddaughter of Robert Smith, the farm's founder. On her death in 1967, the house and its original detached kitchen were relocated to Atlanta History Center by a dedicated group of volunteers with funding from banker Mills B. Lane Jr. Today, the farm contains period buildings brought from other sites in Georgia, including a barn, dairy, smokehouse, cabin, and corncrib, as well as the recreated blacksmith shop and outhouse. The farm also includes garden landscapes consisting of heirloom plants and live animals to help tell the story of 19th-century life.

The farm today includes a restored cabin, interpreted as housing that was common for enslaved laborers who worked on sites like Smith Farm. Robert Smith may have had as many as 19 enslaved people from the time the house was built until emancipation.

Smith Farm Barnyard

The site represents a working slaveholding farm of the Atlanta area in the 1860s. Surrounding the barn and other outbuildings are naturalistic, native plantings. Heritage-breed sheep, goats, chickens, and turkeys also live on the farm.

Tullie Smith House

Robert Hiram Smith, DeKalb County, Georgia, circa 1845

Gift of the Smith Family, 1969

THEO. "TIGER" FLOWERS
Colored Middleweight Champion
World's Most Sensational Boxer
"TIGER" will box MIKE McTIGUE or JOHNNY WILSON
To a Decision Absolutely FREE for any Promoter.
HARRY GREB, GENE TUNNEY, JEFF SMITH, BATTLING SIKI,
can have "TIGERS" end of purse, if he fails to
get as good as a draw.
FLOWERS IS UNCROWNED KING OF MIDDLEWEIGHT
TIGER IS "KING" OF THE JUNGLES IN DIXIE
TIGER LOOKS TO THE EAST FOR PREY
"TIGER" FLOWERS
HOW PANAMA JOE GANS LOST TITLE

Tiger Flowers Poster

Arriving in Atlanta from Brunswick, Georgia, with just 75 cents in his pocket, Theodore "Tiger" Flowers did not look like a future world middleweight boxing champion. He began his professional career at 23, fighting in local arenas, including Atlanta's Municipal Auditorium & Armory. Later, he fought in New York City's Madison Square Garden, where he won his first middleweight title in 1926 in front of 16,000 spectators.

Flowers took pride in his family and his church. He found his calling and community as a deacon—he was known as "The Georgia Deacon"—at Butler Street CME Church in Atlanta. He took his Bible wherever he went, including the boxing ring. He quoted Psalm 144:

> Praise be to the Lord my Rock,
> who trains my hands for war,
> my fingers for battle.
> He is my loving God and my fortress,
> my stronghold and my deliverer,
> my shield, in whom I take refuge,
> who subdues peoples under me.

Flowers also asked the Lord to help him just "a little," because asking for a complete knockout "ain't doing right."

A member of the International Boxing Hall of Fame, Flowers is considered one of the greatest left-hand "southpaws" in boxing history with 115 wins, including 56 knockouts, and only 14 losses. He died in 1927 following minor surgery to correct an injury to his eye, after which 6,000 people filed past his casket in the same city auditorium in which he boxed. The Atlanta street Tiger Flowers Drive is near his former home in west Atlanta.

Promotional Poster

J. Walkington "Walk" Miller, promoter, Atlanta, circa 1926

Purchase with funds from Massey Charitable Trust, 2000

Mi Gente Mural

In 2019, Atlanta History Center partnered with Freedom University, the Latino Community Fund Georgia, the Latin American Association, NCG Cinemas, Northeast Plaza, and Plaza Fiesta to commission a mural to represent the diverse Latino communities in the Atlanta area.

The resulting mural, *Mi Gente* (My People), was designed and executed by Mexican-born artist Yehimi Cambrón, who specializes in public art. Her works have appeared in the Atlanta-area cities of Decatur and Hapeville as well as in Mercedez-Benz Stadium. Through the thematic areas of education, labor, gender, and political advocacy, *Mi Gente* presents five portraits and the foundational vignettes that support them.

Mi Gente was painted on an exterior wall of Northeast Plaza shopping center. The mall is on a 13-mile stretch of Buford Highway where Atlantans and visitors can find one of the most diverse selections of international businesses in the southeastern U.S.

Buford Highway runs through the northeastern metro communities of Brookhaven, Chamblee, Doraville, and Norcross. Other Buford Highway strip malls, such as Plaza Fiesta, often serve as community gathering spaces for celebrations of cultural heritage, concerts, and more.

Mi Gente
Yehimi Cambrón, artist, 2019
Mural made possible by a donation from Thalia & Michael C. Carlos Foundation, 2019

here to stay
MI GENTE
YEHIMI CAMB
ATLANTA HIST
EXIT ONLY
EXIT ONLY

Civil War Presentation Sword

Major General Patrick R. Cleburne was one of the most famous commanders in the Confederate Army of Tennessee, which defended Atlanta during the Civil War.

Soldiers of the 15th Arkansas Infantry presented Cleburne with this dress sword on April 18, 1864. Using a blade made in Solingen, Prussia, Atlanta dentist and jewelry maker Hammond Marshall embellished the sword with the state seal of Arkansas, Cleburne's adopted home. The scabbard also features a harp, the national symbol of Ireland, Cleburne's native country.

On November 30, 1864, the Army of Tennessee was ordered to charge the fortified Union defenses at Franklin, Tennessee. After protesting the ill-advised order, Cleburne reportedly remarked, "Well, if we are to die, let us die like men." His body was found 40 yards from the Union lines.

The sword survived because Cleburne had left it in camp before entering the battle. Cleburne's staff sent the sword to his fiancée, Susan Tarleton, in Alabama. It remained in the Tarleton family until 1944. It was discovered in an umbrella stand in a New England antique store in the 1950s, after which it was purchased and donated to Atlanta History Center.

Presentation Sword

Unidentified maker, Solingen, Prussia, circa 1864;
H. Marshall & Company, engraver, Atlanta, 1864
Gift of Beverly M. DuBose III in honor of his father Beverly M. DuBose Jr., 1986

Margaret Mitchell Marsh

Mrs. John Marsh, the Atlanta-born holder of this city library card, was an avid reader better known as Margaret Mitchell. As a child, Mitchell told tales before she learned to read and later filled notebooks with stories and plays. During her time studying at Smith College in Massachusetts, Mitchell was known by her nickname, Peggy. When she joined the writing staff of the *Atlanta Journal* in 1922, her byline was "Peggy Mitchell."

The 1936 publication of her novel *Gone With the Wind* made "Margaret Mitchell" famous overnight and pushed Atlanta into the global spotlight. The story of resilience in a time of war captivated readers, broke sales records, won the Pulitzer Prize, and was translated into more than 40 languages. Despite the book's popularity, it was not universally accepted. From the moment of its publication, *Gone With the Wind* sparked controversy about its portrayal of the Civil War and its aftermath, a portrayal that promoted ideology related to the Lost Cause and racially charged stereotypes about Reconstruction.

The 1939 movie premiere at Atlanta's Loew's Grand Theatre brought Hollywood royalty to Peachtree Street and put Atlanta on the national stage. In 1940, the film adaptation of Mitchell's book was presented with 10 Academy Awards. It remains one of the most commercially successful movies ever made.

Mitchell created vivid characters recognizable by a single name—Scarlett, Rhett, Ashley, Mammy, and more. The fame that came with a best-selling novel left Mitchell overwhelmed with requests for public engagements. She sought a more private life, preferring to be known simply as "Mrs. John Marsh." In 1949, Margaret Mitchell died at Grady Hospital from injuries sustained when a car struck her while she crossed Peachtree Street. This wallet was in the purse she carried that evening.

Margaret Mitchell's Wallet, Driver's License, and Library Card

Purchase with funds for Margaret Mitchell House, 2022

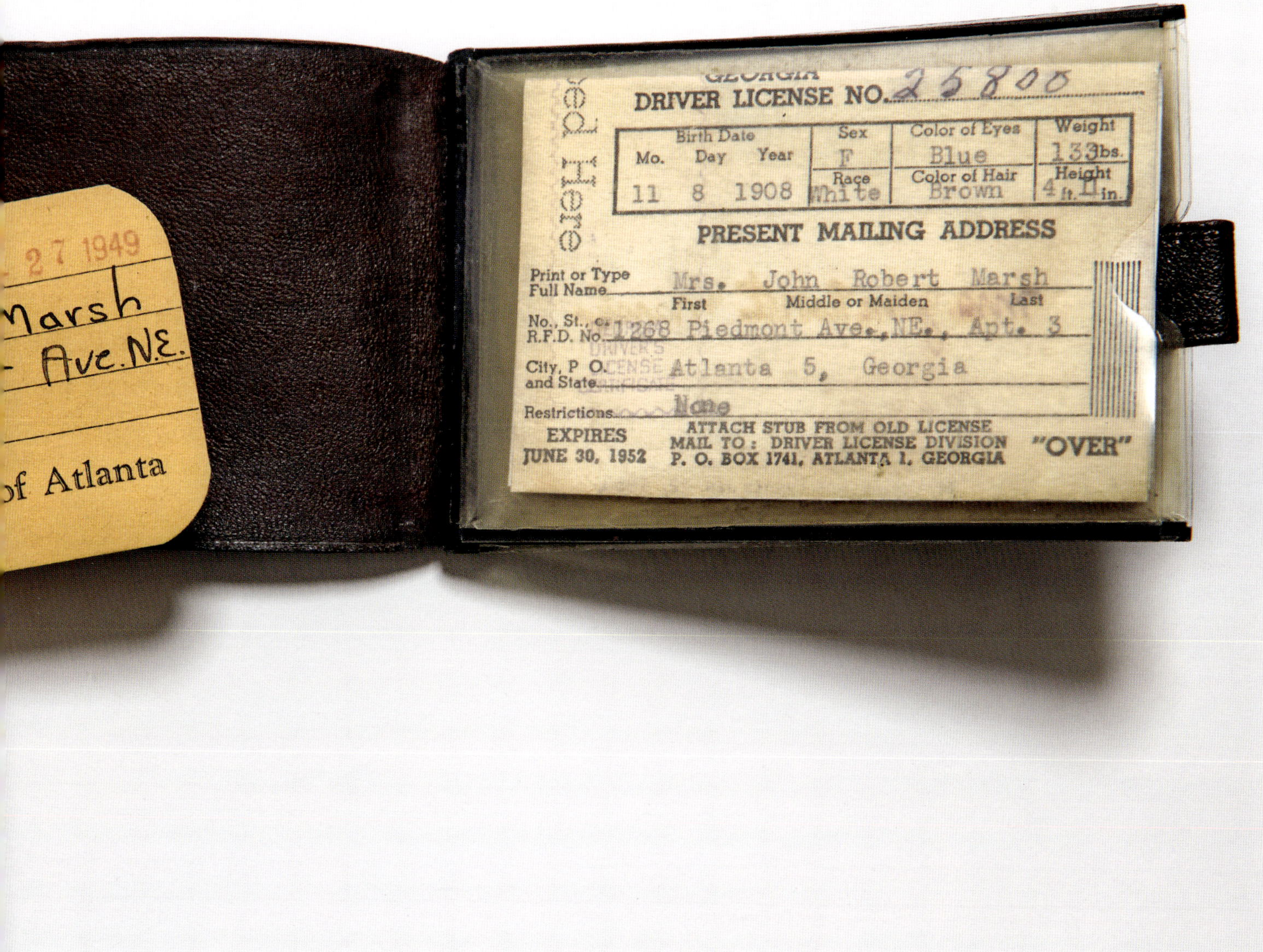
27 1949
Marsh
Ave. N.E.
of Atlanta
GEORGIA
DRIVER LICENSE NO. 25800
Birth Date
Mo. Day Year
11 8 1908
Sex
F
Race
White
Color of Eyes
Blue
Color of Hair
Brown
Weight
133 lbs.
Height
4 ft. 11 in.
PRESENT MAILING ADDRESS
Print or Type Full Name
Mrs. John Robert Marsh
First Middle or Maiden Last
No., St., or R.F.D. No.
1268 Piedmont Ave., NE., Apt. 3
City, P. O. and State
Atlanta 5, Georgia
Restrictions
None
EXPIRES JUNE 30, 1952
ATTACH STUB FROM OLD LICENSE
MAIL TO: DRIVER LICENSE DIVISION
P. O. BOX 1741, ATLANTA 1, GEORGIA
"OVER"

WAR CORRESPONDENT
U.S.

Wright Bryan Jacket and Cap

In June 1944, radio listeners in Atlanta and around the U.S. heard journalist Wright Bryan's report on the parachute landing of the first Allied forces into occupied France. The D-Day invasion had begun. With his soft Southern accent, Wright provided the first eyewitness report on the invasion.

Bryan lived and worked with troops as a war correspondent for Atlanta's WSB radio and NBC news, wearing this jacket during his service. Commonly called "tanker" jackets, these were a component of the U.S. Army winter combat uniform, originally designed for armored vehicle crews.

On the June 6 flight across the English Channel with the Air Force's 9th Troop Carrier Command, parachutists of the 101st Airborne Division waited as air rushed in the open back door. "I watched from the rear door of our plane, named the Snooty, as 17 American parachutists jumped with their arms, ammunition, and equipment into German occupied France," Wright told listeners. The plane was over France for just 11 minutes. The parachutists exited the plane in just over 10 seconds.

Back in Georgia during World War II, civilians saw local changes when the nation rallied for war. Many people found jobs in wartime industries, especially women workers, and mingled with troops from around the country at military bases. This response to the war pushed Georgia into the modern era with associated economic and social changes.

Bryan was wounded and captured by the German army in late 1944, spending six months as a prisoner of war until freed in early 1945. After his service in Europe, Bryan returned to his role as managing editor of the *Atlanta Journal*.

Tanker Jacket
Unidentified maker,
circa 1943
Gift of Wright Bryan III, 2008

Service Cap
Brooks Brothers,
New York, circa 1945
Gift of E. Newell Bryan Tozzer, 2008

The Great Atlanta Fire

On a windy day in May 1917, firemen guided a team of two horses pulling a steam-powered fire engine toward Auburn Avenue to battle a blaze late into the night. Sparks from an unknown source near the city's Oakland Cemetery ignited a fire that destroyed 2,000 homes, altered Atlanta neighborhoods, and spurred the transition to a fully motorized fleet of fire trucks.

The fire engine, named the *Steve R. Johnston*, carried coal and kindling for fuel. Upon arrival at a fire scene, the firemen had to wait for steam to build up in the engine before they could pump the water. Crews of firemen, using a mix of motorized and steam-powered fire engines, failed to stop the fire from spreading. As the fire approached Ponce de Leon Avenue, almost two miles north of its starting point, firemen created a firebreak on the wide avenue by dynamiting 20 homes, remembered as "stately mansions." More than 10 hours later, the fire was halted at last.

By nightfall, 50 city blocks had suffered damage, and refugees sheltered in the homes of friends, churches, and public buildings. Hundreds of people slept in Piedmont Park, Atlanta's largest public space, which was located only a short distance from the edge of the fire.

Atlanta's rebuilding process was affected by racial segregation. Both Black and white neighborhoods had been destroyed, but white neighborhoods were much wealthier and their residents were able to rebuild and find temporary shelter more easily than their Black counterparts. Black families left the overcrowded Auburn Avenue area, moving west near Black academic institutions, including Morehouse College and Spelman Seminary.

"Metropolitan" Horse-drawn Steam Fire Engine, No. 3329
American LaFrance Fire Engine Company, Elmira, New York, circa 1911
Gift of Steve B. Campbell, 1993

R. JOHNSTON

Georgia Real Estate, Loan & Trust Company

At the end of the 19th century, Black entrepreneurs pursued new business opportunities available to them. Georgia Real Estate, Loan & Trust Company was among the most ambitious of these enterprises. The signatures on company certificates reflect the ability of Black businessman and Republican politician Henry A. Rucker to attract a mix of white and Black investors.

Construction of the Rucker Building in 1906 with the resulting profits demonstrates his success. Located on Auburn Avenue, it was the first Black-owned office building in Atlanta and became an important cornerstone of the Black community.

In addition to success in real estate, Rucker made contributions in other business and political arenas, including serving as Georgia's federal tax collector. His entry into real estate investing in 1890 fits a pattern among Black businessmen of the time, who were able to find success with enterprises catering to powerful white clientele.

As the owner of a popular barbershop in downtown Atlanta, Rucker counted wealthy white leaders among his customers. Turning them into investors helped Rucker collect large amounts of capital at a time when few Black families had additional money for investments.

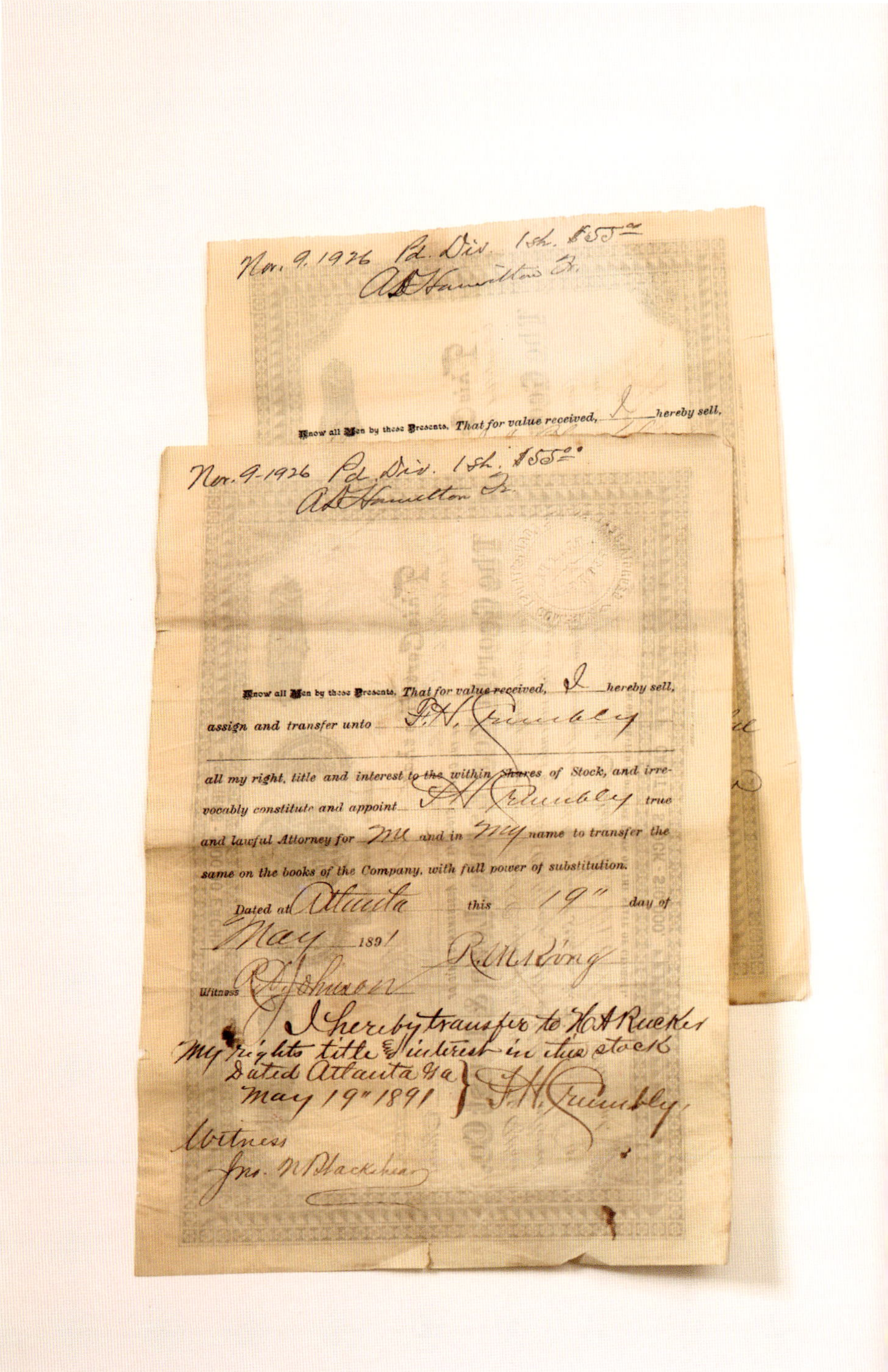

Stock Certificates
Georgia Real Estate, Loan & Trust Company, Atlanta, 1890–1891
Gift of Lucy Rucker Aiken, 1980

SOUTHERN
SLEEPING CAR
PORTER

Railroad Porter Hat

When Willie Leonard Sims of Atlanta put on this Pullman porter hat, he was not just going to work, he was participating in one of the most significant political, economic, and social shifts of the 20th century. The Pullman Company hired Black men as porters and women as maids to assist travelers in luxury sleeping cars on the company's trains. The porters and maids worked grueling hours, faced harassment and racial discrimination, and sleep was allowed only "where requirements of the service permit."

The job, however, was desirable because its pay afforded the employee's family the security of a middle-class lifestyle. As the porters passed through communities, they brought with them Black-owned newspapers containing information on jobs and housing, as well as safe places to travel. As Black migrants made their way North searching for work and a better life, these newspapers, passed on by Pullman porters, proved invaluable.

Pullman service employees began to organize in 1925 as the Brotherhood of Sleeping Car Porters and Maids. With the leadership of A. Philip Randolph, the Brotherhood fought for better wages and fair treatment. In 1935, the Brotherhood secured federal recognition as a union and in 1937 signed a collective bargaining agreement with the Pullman Company. Their union would be a first for Black workers. The lessons learned in the fight for unionization were used again during the Civil Rights Movement when A. Philip Randolph chaired the 1963 March on Washington.

Porter's Hat
Ruby's Uniform Caps, Chicago, circa 1942
Purchase with funds for the Collections, 2024

1906 Atlanta Race Massacre

On Saturday, September 22, 1906, thousands of angry white Atlantans gathered at the corner of Pryor and Decatur Streets in downtown Atlanta. Fueled by false, sensationalized reports of Black men brutalizing white women, many who gathered there sought to attack anyone who was Black. The violent mob assaulted hundreds of Black Atlantans and their businesses in the city's central commercial district into the night and over the following two days.

The City of Atlanta death records document some of those killed that day. At 32 Peachtree Street, members of the mob shot a Black barber at work. Other victims include a schoolboy of 13, who died from his injuries after being taken to the city's Grady Hospital, and an 18-year-old messenger who died of stab wounds.

A correspondent for the London-based *Morning Post* reported, "Sixteen blacks are known to have been killed, while the bodies of many of the dead were smuggled out of the town to save them from indignities at the hands of the uncontrollable whites." Official reports in 1906 underestimated the number killed. White city leaders sought to downplay the violence, which challenged the image of Atlanta as a progressive and modern "New South" city.

Many details of the massacre remain unknown. Although the city coroner issued only 10 death certificates for Black victims, modern historians agree that at least 25 Black Atlantans were murdered, hundreds were wounded, and many Black businesses and homes were burned or destroyed. While Black Atlantans would not forget the terror, the massacre was minimized for decades in the white community and ignored in official histories of the city.

Deaths, 1906
City of Atlanta, 1906
Courtesy City of Atlanta, 2023

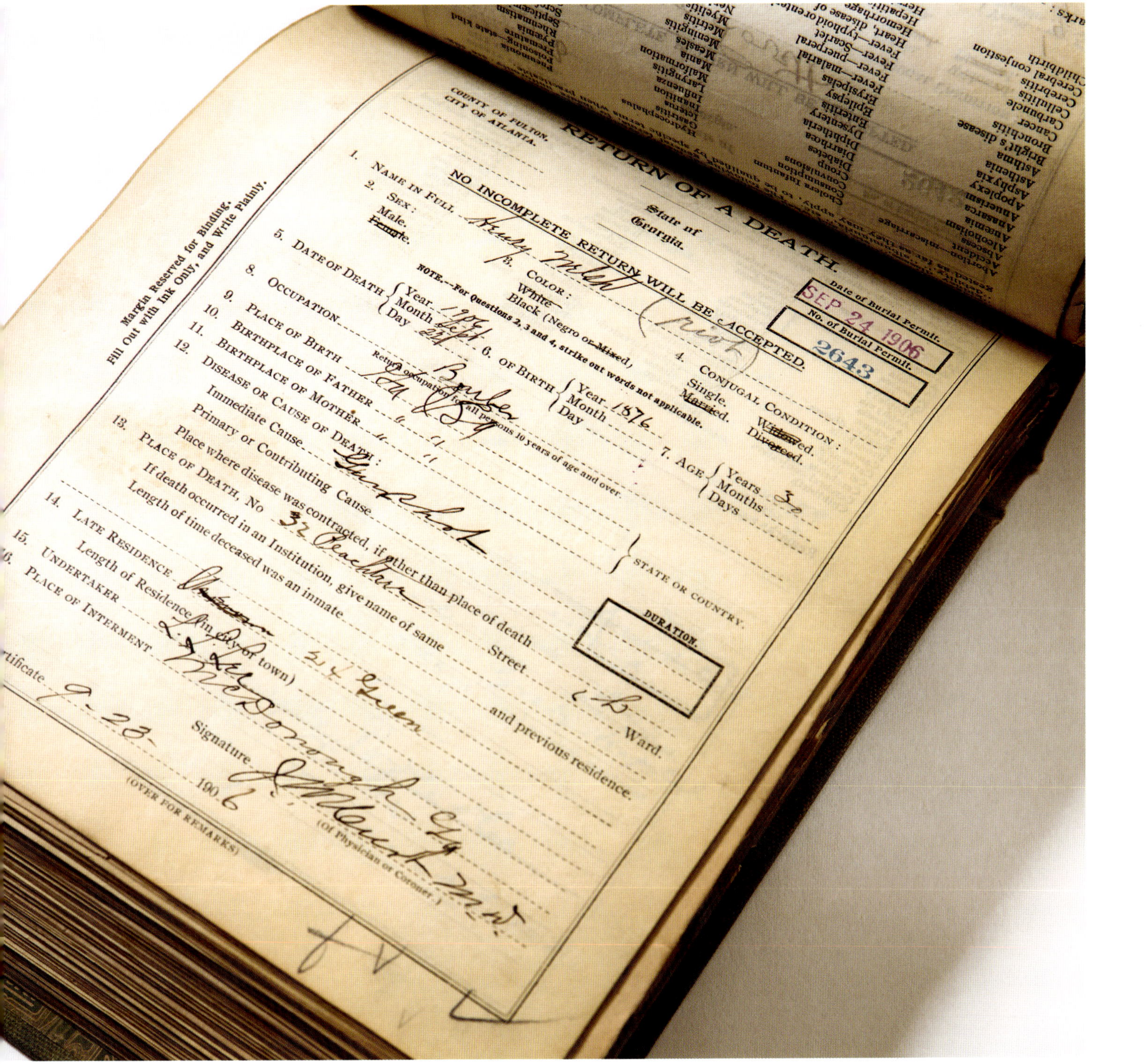
COUNTY OF FULTON,
CITY OF ATLANTA.

RETURN OF A DEATH.

State of Georgia.

NO INCOMPLETE RETURN WILL BE ACCEPTED.

Date of Burial Permit. SEP 24 1906
No. of Burial Permit. 2643

Margin Reserved for Binding.
Fill Out with Ink Only, and Write Plainly.

1. NAME IN FULL Henry Miller (riot)
2. SEX: Male. ~~Female~~.
3. COLOR: White Black (Negro or ~~Mixed~~),
4. CONJUGAL CONDITION: Single. ~~Married~~. Widowed. ~~Divorced~~.

NOTE.—For Questions 2, 3 and 4, strike out words not applicable.

5. DATE OF DEATH { Year 1906 Month Sept Day 22
6. DATE OF BIRTH { Year 1876 Month Day
7. AGE { Years 30 Months Days
8. OCCUPATION Barber
Return occupation for all persons 10 years of age and over.
9. PLACE OF BIRTH Atl Ga
10. BIRTHPLACE OF FATHER " "
11. BIRTHPLACE OF MOTHER " "
} STATE OR COUNTRY.
12. DISEASE OR CAUSE OF DEATH: Gun Shot
Immediate Cause.
Primary or Contributing Cause.
Place where disease was contracted, if other than place of death
DURATION.
13. PLACE OF DEATH, No 32 Peachtree Street Ward
If death occurred in an Institution, give name of same
Length of time deceased was an inmate
14. LATE RESIDENCE ~~Unknown~~ 21 Green and previous residence.
Length of Residence (in city or town) L. L. Lee
15. UNDERTAKER
16. PLACE OF INTERMENT McDonough Ga
Certificate 9-23- 1906 Signature. J. Mack M.D.
(Of Physician or Coroner.)
(OVER FOR REMARKS)

HASTINGS' NURSERY ANNUAL
WINTER 1930-1931
3 NEW ROSE SENSATIONS
$3.35 POST PAID
VILLE DE PARIS $1 EACH
MISS ROWENA THOM $1.50 EACH
HAIRY VETCH
Fall 1913
HASTINGS SEEDS
Catalogue No. 46
CRIMSON CLOVER
100 BUSHEL OATS
CATALOGUE № 38
SUMMER AND FALL
1909
HASTINGS' SEEDS
H·G·HASTINGS & CO·
16 WEST MITCHELL ST
ATLANTA GEORGIA.

Hastings' Seeds Catalogs

In the early 20th century, the arrival of seed catalogs each winter signaled the return of spring. Vibrant colors, delightful descriptions, and enviable gardens greeted the reader. The catalogs were filled with endless possibilities and included suggestions and valuable information on varieties; growing requirements; planting schedules; and insight into trends in Southern farming, gardening, and landscape design.

In 1899, H.G. Hastings & Company, which focused on Southern agricultural farmers and home gardeners, moved to Atlanta from Florida. Atlanta offered convenient distribution to grow their mail-order seed business that focused on integrity and delivering superior products.

By 1940, Hastings had moved its offices and storefront to Marietta Street near downtown Atlanta. During World War II, Hastings and a number of other seed companies helped Victory Gardens flourish.

Hastings provided guidance and confidence to home gardeners for decades. It connected with urban and rural customers, building a loyal following and adding an array of plants to the Atlanta landscape. The business remained family-owned until it was sold in 1976.

The Hastings Company collection includes seed catalogs from 1889 to 1993 along with the company records. The collection is part of the Cherokee Garden Library, one of the special collection libraries of Atlanta History Center's Kenan Research Center. Founded in 1975, the library is named for the state floral emblem of Georgia, the Cherokee rose.

Seed Catalogs

Atlanta: H.G. Hastings & Company, 1901–1931

Gift of Donald M. Hastings Jr. and Chris Hastings, 2002

SAMUEL SPENCER
1847 - 1906

Samuel Spencer Statue

Samuel Spencer, president of Southern Railway, was one of the most successful Southern businessmen of his time. He made Atlanta the hub of the Southern Railway network, which included 7,500 miles of track. When he was killed in a train accident in 1906, employees pooled their resources to memorialize the man who helped create one of the dominant railroad systems in the South. An estimated 30,000 railway employees—nearly three-quarters of the workforce—contributed to the fund to honor Spencer.

The memorial committee selected the preeminent public sculptor of the era, Daniel Chester French, to create the statue. French is famous for his 1920 sculpture of President Abraham Lincoln, housed in the Lincoln Memorial in Washington, D.C. French created the statue of Spencer in 1909–1910 at his studio in Massachusetts. The Tennessee marble base was designed by Henry Bacon, the future architect of the Lincoln Memorial building.

Southern Railway gave French's Spencer statue a prominent place on the heavily traveled plaza of Atlanta's Terminal Station, one of the city's two main train stations, from 1910 to 1970. Later, it was placed in front of the headquarters of Norfolk Southern (the descendant of the Southern Railway Company). In 2023, the City of Atlanta licensed the memorial to Atlanta History Center. It is now used to promote discussion about Samuel Spencer, the importance of railroads to Atlanta's growth, public art, and the complex legacies of the Old and New South.

Samuel Spencer Memorial

Daniel Chester French, sculptor, Chesterwood Studio, Stockbridge, Massachusetts, 1910

Courtesy City of Atlanta, 2023

161

Order granted G. Schaumburger for beef and mutton furnished Barheone $64.92. S. J. Craft for fixing embankment on Pope street $22.50. J. M. H. Forgason for work of lay on street in 1850. $4.50

The bill of Messrs Mennings & Blackburn Cannarti, H. K. & A. J. King were referred to Deputy Marsh for investigation.

The statement of Mr Lyon Malamp respecting the ...ship of Mr Clapp was read and on motion it ... resolved that he have an order for $4.50 and he receive that amount per week for attendance to ...lapp

...inance was adopted prohibiting the burning ...ank kiln within a certain distance of the ...nce of any citizen

Council then adjourned

25 July 1851

...the Mayor, Aldermen Jones Hayden

...meeting read & approved

...from divers citizens pray...tion concerning the erec... square by the officers ... on motion ordered to

...king coffin $2.50 ... to Wm Henry ... for their ...

Present his honor the ... McShaffrey Jones & Adams...

Order granted J. M. Rac... 4th Inst $6.00 in lieu of ... June last.

The statement of Mr. McConn... pected insurrection of certain ... on motion it was Resolved That ... viz Henry Long, Peter Huff, Ha... Burrell, Stephen Cannark, Kennis... Levi & him, be arrested by the Ma... the council meet in session ... to investigate the charge against ...

A motion was carried appointing ...

Council then a...

1 August 1851

Present his honor the Mayor; Aldermen Humph... McShaffrey Mayse and Rourk

Resolved that the clerk be authori... draw on such ... by the Mayor

The bill of Messrs ... miller on ...

Resol...

Atlanta City Council Minutes

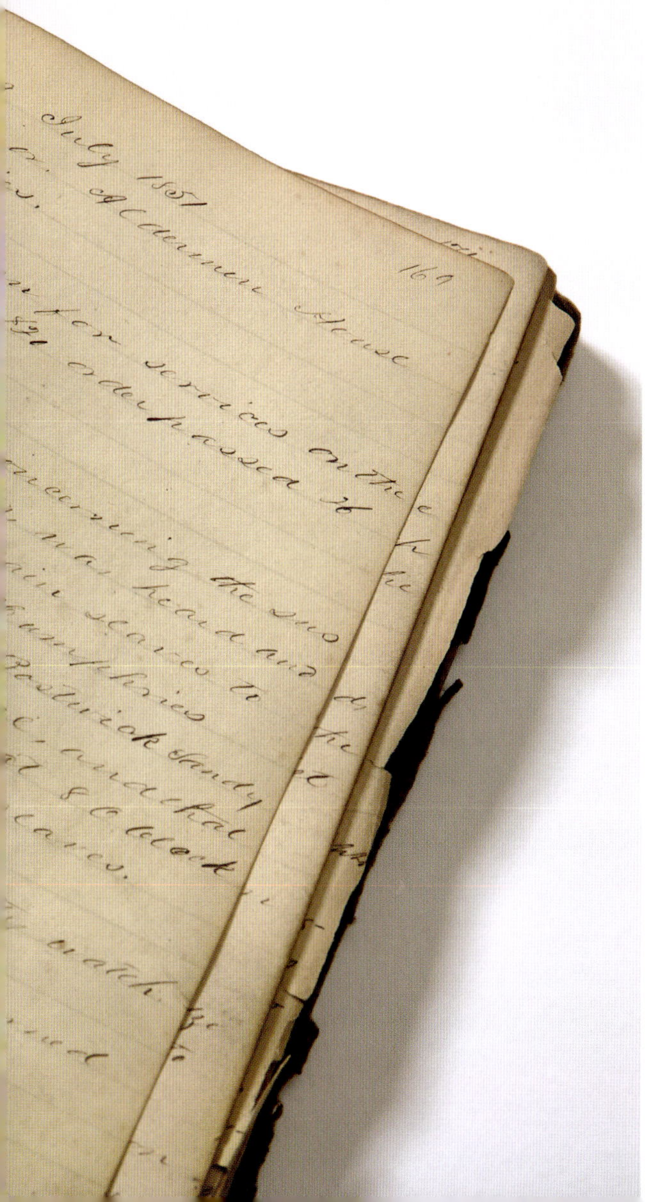

As these meeting minutes show, the 1851 Atlanta city council, meeting just four years after the creation of the new city of Atlanta, tackled various issues common to Southern cities of the time. Among references to the mundane business of cityhood—digging wells and establishing a graveyard—is the mention of "a suspected insurrection of certain slaves."

The council resolved that day to arrest at least seven men based on the accusation, but no record exists of what happened to the accused. Throughout the South, restrictive laws controlled the lives of enslaved people to prevent resistance. For the nearly 500 enslaved people living in Atlanta in the early 1850s, life was one of oppressive legal codes and heavy regulation.

The legal status of free Black persons—numbering around 20 individuals in the 1850 census—was only marginally better than their enslaved brethren. While the rapidly growing city of Atlanta benefited from the labor provided by enslaved people, their presence represented a risk.

The mention in the council minutes of "suspected insurrection" reflects a common fear among Southern slaveholders: enslaved people coming together and violently resisting being held in bondage.

Atlanta City Council Minutes Book
February 2, 1848–July 22, 1852
Courtesy City of Atlanta, 1969

John Abbot

In 1776, a young Englishman arrived in Georgia ready to record the plant and insect life of the New World. During his 64 years in Georgia, John Abbot produced thousands of drawings of birds, butterflies, moths, and plants, creating the largest record of the early Southeast by an artist-naturalist.

Abbot explored the swamps bordering the Ogeechee River; Piney Woods near the Savannah River; and the countryside of Burke, Chatham, and Bulloch Counties between Augusta and Savannah. He captured insects along cultivated fields and noted changes in plant and bird life as settlers transformed much of the existing landscapes into farmland.

Abbot's childhood fascination with insects and his "taste for drawing" gave him the curiosity and tools needed for his occupation. He sent both specimens and drawings to his London-based dealer, who sold them to collectors, often crediting the source as simply his "correspondent in Georgia."

Abbot's drawings remained largely in private hands. In 1797, James Edward Smith brought 104 of Abbot's images to a larger audience in *The Natural History of the Rarer Lepidopterous Insects of Georgia*. Hand-colored engravings created from Abbot's watercolor drawings document the life cycle of moths and butterflies, as well as the plants on which they lived near Abbot's rural Georgia home.

Today, visitors to Goizueta Gardens at Atlanta History Center can find many of the native plants recorded in Abbot's book, including pinxterbloom azalea (*Rhododendron periclymenoides*), sweet shrub (*Calycanthus floridus*), blue-eyed grass (*Sisyrinchium angustifolium*), sweetgum (*Liquidambar styraciflua*), and American wisteria (*Wisteria frutescens*).

The Natural History of the Rarer Lepidopterous Insects of Georgia

London: Printed by T. Bensley for J. Edwards, Volumes 1 and 2, 1797

Gift to the Cherokee Garden Library from Dr. Carl R. Hartrampf Jr. in honor of Patricia Crawford Hartrampf, 2017

91
TAB. XLVI.
PHALÆNA PROMETHEA.
SMALLER DARK-BROWN EMPEROR MOTH.
187
TAB. XCIV.
PHALÆNA OBLINITA.
SMEARED, OR COTTON MOTH.
GOSSYPIUM BARBADENSE. LINN.
BARBADOES COTTON.
Ph. Noctua fpirilinguis criftata, alis lanceolatis canis punctis nigris marginem verfus effluentibus.
This caterpillar feeds on the Cotton, Willow, and feveral water plants. It enclofed itfelf in a white web on the leaves November 6th, and came out the 7th of April. Others went through their changes in fummer. Though not very common, it is found in Virginia as well as Georgia.
The fpecies before us has much affinity to the Shark Moth, Ph. umbratica. It is well diftinguifhed by the black fpots on the difk of the upper wings appearing as if they had been partly wafhed or fmeared off.

World Globe

Donated to Atlanta's Carnegie Library in 1950 by Rich's department store, this world globe was a feature until 1977 when the beaux-arts library was demolished to make way for a new building. The sphere was handmade by Replogle Globes and contains an incredible 22,000 place names. The city of Atlanta is missing from the globe, rubbed clean to the metal surface by thousands of library visitors.

The Replogle company was founded in 1930 and found success with a globe made for Marshall Field & Company department store for the Chicago World's Fair, the Century of World Progress International Exposition, in 1933.

In Atlanta, Rich's department store had a long history of philanthropy and involvement in the local community. The donation of the globe to Carnegie Library is an example of Rich's generosity and investment in the city.

By 1977, Atlanta had outgrown the Carnegie Library. Efforts were made to save the building, but in the end, it was demolished and world-famous Hungarian architect Marcel Breuer created the Brutalist design of today's Central Library of the Fulton County Public Library System.

Replogle 32-inch Library Globe
Replogle Globes, Chicago, circa 1950
Gift of William W. Bryan, 2004

CANADA
QUEBEC
ONTARIO
MANITOBA
UNITED STATES OF AMERICA
Detroit
Chicago
Toronto
Ottawa
Montreal
Boston
New York
Philadelphia
Charleston
Savannah
Jacksonville
Tampa
Miami
New Orleans
GULF OF MEXICO
Habana
CUBA
JAMAICA
HAITI
DOMINICAN REP.
HONDURAS
NICARAGUA
CENTRAL AMERICA
MEXICO
HUDSON BAY
Hamilton Bermuda Is.
ATLANTIC
WEST INDIES

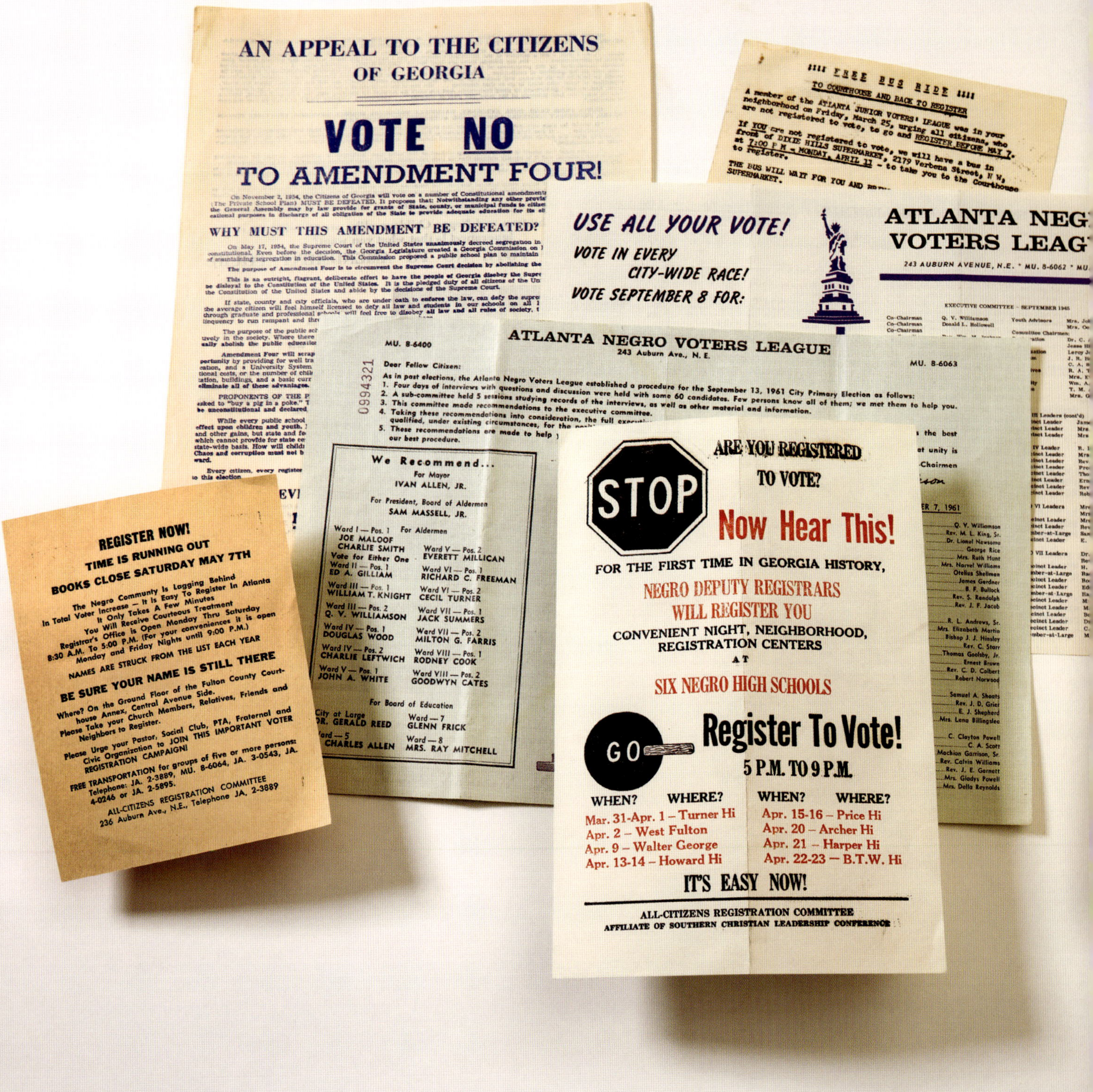
AN APPEAL TO THE CITIZENS OF GEORGIA
VOTE NO
TO AMENDMENT FOUR!
WHY MUST THIS AMENDMENT BE DEFEATED?
FREE BUS RIDE
TO COURTHOUSE AND BACK TO REGISTER
USE ALL YOUR VOTE!
VOTE IN EVERY CITY-WIDE RACE!
VOTE SEPTEMBER 8 FOR:
ATLANTA NEGRO VOTERS LEAGUE
243 Auburn Ave., N. E.
MU. 8-6400
MU. 8-6063
Dear Fellow Citizen:
We Recommend...
For Mayor
IVAN ALLEN, JR.
For President, Board of Aldermen
SAM MASSELL, JR.
For Aldermen
Ward I — Pos. 1 JOE MALOOF
CHARLIE SMITH
Ward V — Pos. 2 EVERETT MILLICAN
Ward II — Pos. 1 ED A. GILLIAM
Ward VI — Pos. 1 RICHARD C. FREEMAN
Ward III — Pos. 1 WILLIAM T. KNIGHT
Ward VI — Pos. 2 CECIL TURNER
Ward III — Pos. 2 Q. V. WILLIAMSON
Ward VII — Pos. 1 JACK SUMMERS
Ward IV — Pos. 1 DOUGLAS WOOD
Ward VII — Pos. 2 MILTON G. FARRIS
Ward IV — Pos. 2 CHARLIE LEFTWICH
Ward VIII — Pos. 1 RODNEY COOK
Ward V — Pos. 1 JOHN A. WHITE
Ward VIII — Pos. 2 GOODWYN CATES
For Board of Education
Ward — 7 GLENN FRICK
Ward — 5 CHARLES ALLEN
Ward — 8 MRS. RAY MITCHELL
REGISTER NOW!
TIME IS RUNNING OUT
BOOKS CLOSE SATURDAY MAY 7TH
NAMES ARE STRUCK FROM THE LIST EACH YEAR
BE SURE YOUR NAME IS STILL THERE
ALL-CITIZENS REGISTRATION COMMITTEE
236 Auburn Ave., N.E., Telephone JA. 2-3889
ARE YOU REGISTERED TO VOTE?
STOP
Now Hear This!
FOR THE FIRST TIME IN GEORGIA HISTORY,
NEGRO DEPUTY REGISTRARS
WILL REGISTER YOU
CONVENIENT NIGHT, NEIGHBORHOOD, REGISTRATION CENTERS
AT
SIX NEGRO HIGH SCHOOLS
GO
Register To Vote!
5 P.M. TO 9 P.M.
WHEN? WHERE?
Mar. 31-Apr. 1 – Turner Hi
Apr. 2 – West Fulton
Apr. 9 – Walter George
Apr. 13-14 – Howard Hi
WHEN? WHERE?
Apr. 15-16 – Price Hi
Apr. 20 – Archer Hi
Apr. 21 – Harper Hi
Apr. 22-23 – B.T.W. Hi
IT'S EASY NOW!
ALL-CITIZENS REGISTRATION COMMITTEE
AFFILIATE OF SOUTHERN CHRISTIAN LEADERSHIP CONFERENCE

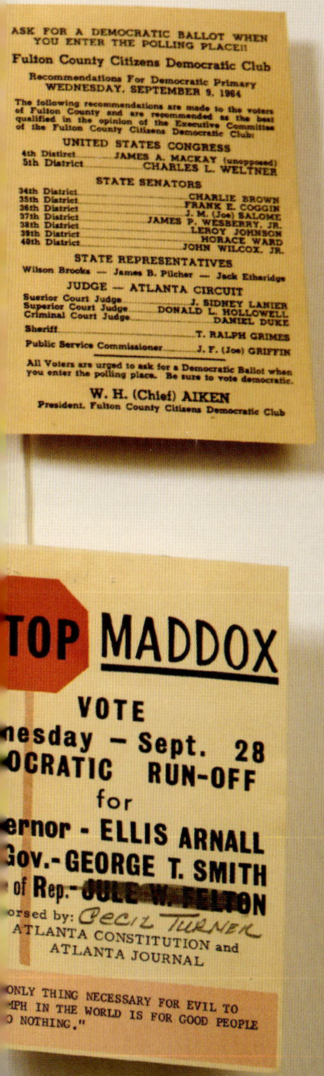

Black Voter Registration

In 1870, the ratification of the 15th Amendment guaranteed American men the right to vote regardless of "race, color, or previous condition of servitude." By 1899, however, the all-white Democratic primary had largely disenfranchised Black Georgians. Because Georgia was essentially a one-party state at the time, the Democratic candidate was assured victory in most political races.

In the early 20th century, Atlanta's Black community navigated numerous hurdles further restricting Black voter participation, including poll taxes, literacy tests, and intimidation when trying to register.

Despite these limitations, some Black Atlantans were able to register and made an impact with their votes by influencing bond referendums. Early victories included a 1921 vote to fund the first Black public high school in Atlanta, Booker T. Washington High School.

The 1944 U.S. Supreme Court decision *Smith v. Allwright* outlawed the white primary. In a 1946 special election, energized voter-registration efforts in Atlanta allowed Black voters to help elect the second woman to represent Georgia in Congress, Helen Douglas Mankin. Mankin was the only candidate to seek Black support, and the votes cast in Black precincts secured her victory.

As voting barriers continued to be overturned into the 1950s and 1960s, Black Atlantans were given flyers such as these, promising, "You will receive courteous treatment" and the opportunity to be registered by a "Negro Registrar." A postcard reminded potential voters that registering "is absolutely free."

Voter Registration Materials

Atlanta: All Citizens Registration Committee, Atlanta Negro Voter's League, Fulton County Citizens Democratic League, and Georgia Teachers and Education Association, 1954–1965

Gifts of Lucy Rucker Aiken, 1980, and Jenelsie Walden Holloway, 1988

Victorian-period Dresses

During the late 19th century, women's fashion reflected social and technological changes that influenced the design and color of women's clothing.

Sleeves that had grown enormous—pagoda sleeves—became thin again, the hoop skirt gave way to a slimmer skirt, and the female form assumed new proportions with the popularity of the bustle.

Some of the color examples here possibly use aniline, a chemical dye invented in the 1850s. Fashion designers were quick to apply what previously had been impossible colors, like the magenta in this 1871 dress worn by Emma Moore Draper, cited as "one of Atlanta's best known women" at her death in 1910.

The 1868 taffeta gown is interesting for its brilliant green, possibly the color known as Paris Green. The coloring was introduced in the early 19th century—its primary component was arsenic. The dress posed little harm to the wearer as long as she wore her undergarments.

These dresses from Atlanta History Center's extensive fashion collection are from a transitional period in which fashion changed from the broad hoop-skirt crinoline to the bustle silhouette. By the late 1880s, the size of the bustle extended from the body to the point that it was "large enough to rest a teacup upon."

Victorian-period Designs
Miscellaneous makers, United States, 1868–1885
Gifts of Mrs. Henry Wilbur Barnes, 1977; Estate of Jesse Draper, 1973; John T. Ferguson, 1968; Florence Griffin, 1980; and Eleanor Buren Hartshorn, 1988

Sherman's Photographer George N. Barnard

Photographer George N. Barnard is best known for his book *Photographic Views of Sherman's Campaign*, which contains scenes of Major General William T. Sherman's Civil War military operations in Georgia and South Carolina. Among the book's 61 prints are 13 depicting the city of Atlanta, surrounding fortifications, and area battlefields.

Barnard arrived in Atlanta following its surrender to Sherman's army in September 1864. While troops surveyed roads, rail lines, and geographical features, Barnard photographed Confederate and Union fortifications, city streets, and Atlanta's railyard.

Working with glass negatives, Barnard required a portable field darkroom and time to set up, chemically prepare the plate, expose the image, and develop the negative—all performed on site. Transported in wagons over dirt roads, the glass negatives were always at risk for breakage. His photographs are not enlargements; they are the same size as the glass negative, some as large as 12-by-15 inches.

In November 1864, Sherman ordered his men to destroy Atlanta's military and transportation capabilities. Subsequently, Barnard photographed Union troops wrecking rail lines and the scenes of the ruins. He then accompanied Sherman's troops on the March to the Sea.

Following the war, Barnard returned to the route of Sherman's campaign to photograph scenes he missed during the war. Late in 1866, he published *Photographic Views of Sherman's Campaign*. Atlanta History Center's volume was the personal copy of General Sherman, signed in 1886 by his son Philemon Tecumseh Sherman.

Barnard's Atlanta scenes are icons of the Civil War, capturing the explosive destruction of the Confederate munitions train, the shelled ruins of homes, and the devastation on Peachtree Street and in the city's railyard.

Photographic Views of Sherman's Campaign
George N. Barnard, photographer
New York: Press of Wynkoop & Hallenbeck, 1866
Courtesy of Charles J. Turner Jr., 2024

Photo from nature By G. N. Barnard.

REBEL WORKS IN FRONT OF ATLANTA, GA. No. 3

Alonzo Herndon Barber's Pole

Barber's Pole
Unidentified maker, circa 1890
Courtesy Alonzo F. & Norris B. Herndon Foundation, 2016

In turn-of-the-century Atlanta, this barber's pole marked the location of one of three shops owned by Alonzo Herndon, one of Atlanta's first Black millionaires. In his Peachtree Street location, Herndon and his team of barbers served prominent and powerful white Atlantans in a space remembered for its gold fixtures and crystal chandeliers.

Born enslaved in 1858 in Walton County, Herndon and his mother, Sophenie, worked the land following emancipation, but they saw little opportunity for success as sharecroppers. Selling peanuts and molasses, he raised funds to leave his rural life.

Following his success in the barbering business, Herndon founded Atlanta Life Insurance Company, invested in real estate, and shared his wealth philanthropically. His businesses provided Atlanta's Black community with essential financial building blocks. Atlanta Life Insurance became a landmark of the city's Black business district, the bustling Sweet Auburn neighborhood.

As a community leader, Herndon supported local institutions and charities that advanced Black business and community life, including Atlanta University, the YMCA, orphanages, nurseries, and First Congregational Church. On a national level, Herndon was a founding member of the National Negro Business League and attended the first meeting of the Niagara Movement, formed in 1905 to champion the full political, economic, and social equality of Black Americans.

Architectural Ornament

A terracotta ornament from the roof of Atlanta Terminal Station is one of the few remnants of what was arguably Atlanta's most beautiful railroad passenger station.

In 1895, Southern Railway President Samuel Spencer began to promote the idea of building a new, grand passenger train station in downtown Atlanta. By that time, Atlanta's Union Depot, constructed in 1871, was functionally obsolete. By May 1903, station design work was under way with P. Thornton Marye as lead architect.

Marye's architectural theme for Terminal Station, according to a newspaper account, was "St. Augustine Transplanted." The design of the new station, constructed with gray brick and extensive terracotta, was influenced by 16th-century Spanish Renaissance and Moorish architecture of Spain and western North Africa.

Constructed at the corner of Mitchell and Madison (now Spring) Streets, Terminal Station opened in 1905 to serve several rail lines: Southern Railway, Central of Georgia Railway, and the Atlanta & West Point Railroad. The Seaboard Air Line Railroad began serving the station in 1916. Other railroads, including the Atlanta, Birmingham & Atlantic Railroad, continued to serve the antiquated Union Depot until moving to a new Union Station in 1930.

With the improvements of highway and air travel in the 1950s and 1960s, the number of passenger trains serving Atlanta declined. Terminal Station closed on June 14, 1970, and was demolished in 1972. Its location is now the site of the Richard B. Russell Federal Building.

Architectural Ornament
P. Thornton Marye, architect, 1905
Gift of P.L. Bealy Smith Family in memory of P.L. Bealy Smith, 1991

Blue Ribbon Quilt

For 100 days in fall 1895, nearly one million visitors attended the Cotton States and International Exposition in today's Piedmont Park, enjoying rides, exhibits, and speakers in grand, specially constructed temporary buildings.

Exposition exhibits included quilts. This blue-ribbon-winning quilt, awarded to Caroline Pope Sutton Wilson, displayed her creativity and skill in customizing a traditional pinwheel pattern, known in her family as "Wheel of Fortune." Women used occasions like fairs to demonstrate excellence in domestic skills, and Wilson enjoyed uncommon public recognition.

The Woman's Building reflected a mix of modern and traditional roles for women. In a striking white structure designed by female architect Elise Mercur, women led programs on academic, professional, and artistic topics. Elsewhere, the United Daughters of the Confederacy glorified the Lost Cause and dedicated a day of the exposition to Confederate veterans.

During the 1890s, the South was still struggling to recover from the Civil War. Atlanta newspaper editor Henry Grady spoke of a "New South" economy based on growth in manufacturing and diversified agriculture. Atlanta business leaders planned the Cotton States and International Exposition to highlight the potential of a modern Southern economy and attract Northern investors.

Though the exposition was segregated, Black Atlantans were included with the creation of the Negro Building, showcasing the achievements and progress of Black citizens following emancipation. Booker T. Washington, founder of today's Tuskeegee University, delivered a speech to highlight African American contributions to the Southern economy. His Atlanta Exposition Address controversially argued for prioritizing Black economic empowerment over social integration. All visitors to the fair experienced sometimes contradictory messages as planners sought to celebrate new economic potential while maintaining traditional Southern social traditions.

Pinwheel Pattern Quilt

Caroline Pope Sutton Wilson, Atlanta, 1890

Gift of Mrs. J.R. Harris, 1974

Atlanta Salutes Hank Aaron

In the summer of 1973, Atlanta Braves baseball player Henry "Hank" Aaron was close to breaking Babe Ruth's career record of 714 home runs. Aaron told sports journalists that he was receiving hate mail from senders who thought that a Black man should not break Ruth's record. Aaron also mentioned threats of violence to him and his family.

By the end of the 1973 season, Aaron was one run shy of tying the record. The Atlanta Chamber of Commerce decided that the city should show their support for Aaron's achievement. A record number of billboards were posted around Atlanta with an illustration of a swinging Aaron superimposed over Babe Ruth's profile with the words, "Atlanta Salutes Hank Aaron."

The Braves began the 1974 season in Cincinnati, where Aaron tied Ruth's record on his first swing. Four days later, on April 8, during a home game against the Los Angeles Dodgers, Aaron broke Babe Ruth's record in front of a crowd that was itself record-breaking at Atlanta–Fulton County Stadium.

Vin Scully, the Dodgers' radio broadcaster, encapsulated the record's significance for Aaron and Atlanta: "What a marvelous moment for Atlanta and the state of Georgia; what a marvelous moment for the country and the world. A Black man is getting a standing ovation in the Deep South for breaking a record of an all-time baseball idol. And it is a great moment for all of us, and particularly for Henry Aaron."

This print, never pasted onto a billboard, was saved by Mike Dillon, a member of the installation crew. Dillon cared for it for 50 years before donating it to Atlanta History Center.

Atlanta Salutes Hank Aaron
Billboard artwork, John Findley, artist, Turner Advertising Company, 1974
Gift of Cornelia and Mike Dillon Family, 2024

Braves
44

Civil War Diary

In 1864, 10-year-old Atlanta resident Carrie Berry recorded her experience of the Union Army's siege and occupation of Atlanta with comments that reflected a mix of her perspective as a young girl and the stoicism expressed by civilians in wartime.

From her family home on Harris Street, less than one mile from the heart of downtown, Berry and her four siblings regularly heard the sounds of war: "We can hear the cannons and muskets very plain, but the shells we dread."

She described her fright at an explosion next to her home, writing that her sister "was pale as a corpse and I expect I was too." The family regularly took refuge in the cellar, where Berry occupied her time with household chores like knitting and caring for her siblings.

Berry records her desires, reminding us that she is still a child. In August 1864, she writes, "How I wish the federals would quit shelling us so that we could get out and get some fresh air." Days earlier, she shared that it was her birthday, "But I did not have a cake—times were too hard so I celebrated with ironing."

After the war, Berry and her family remained in Atlanta. She married and raised three children in the city. On her death in 1921, Berry was buried in historic Oakland Cemetery, where many of the Confederate soldiers killed in the battle that she recorded as a child were also laid to rest.

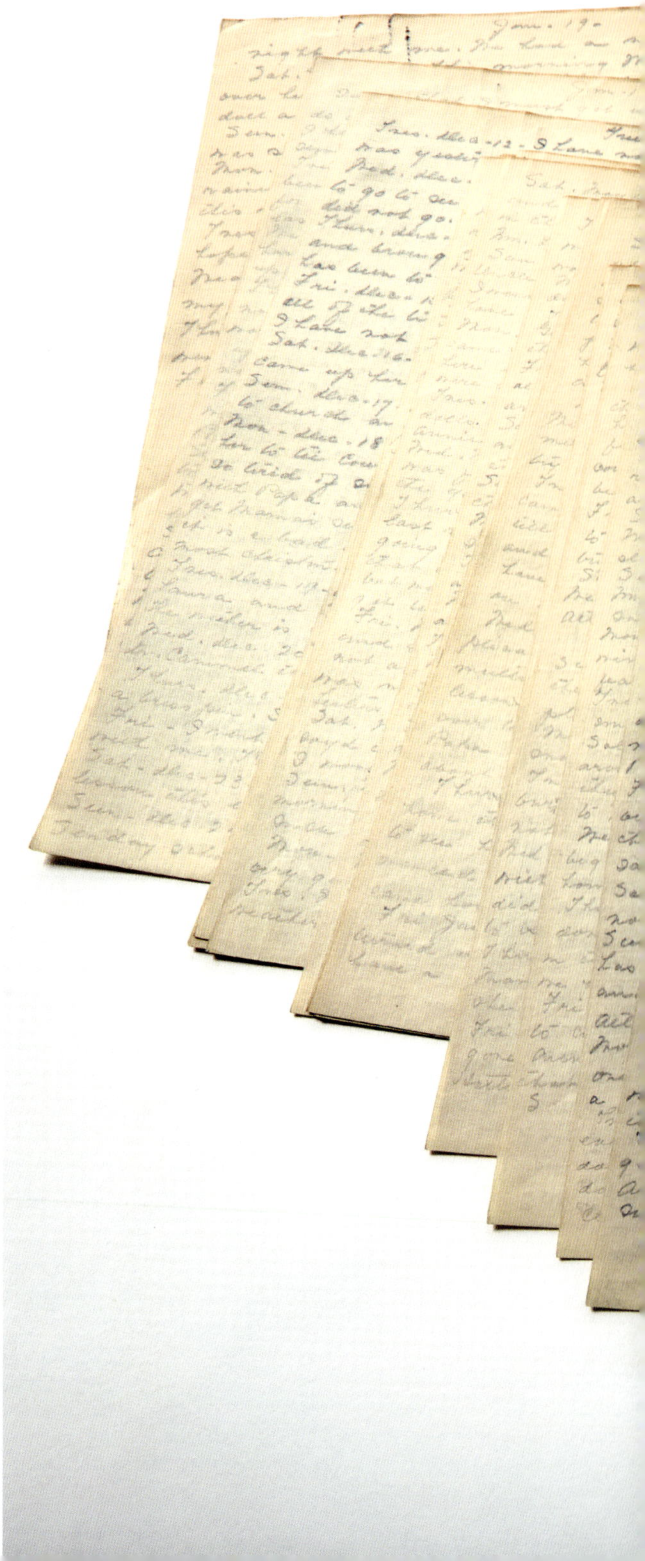

Diary Pages
Carrie Berry, Atlanta, 1864–1865
Gift of Dan Franklin, 1970

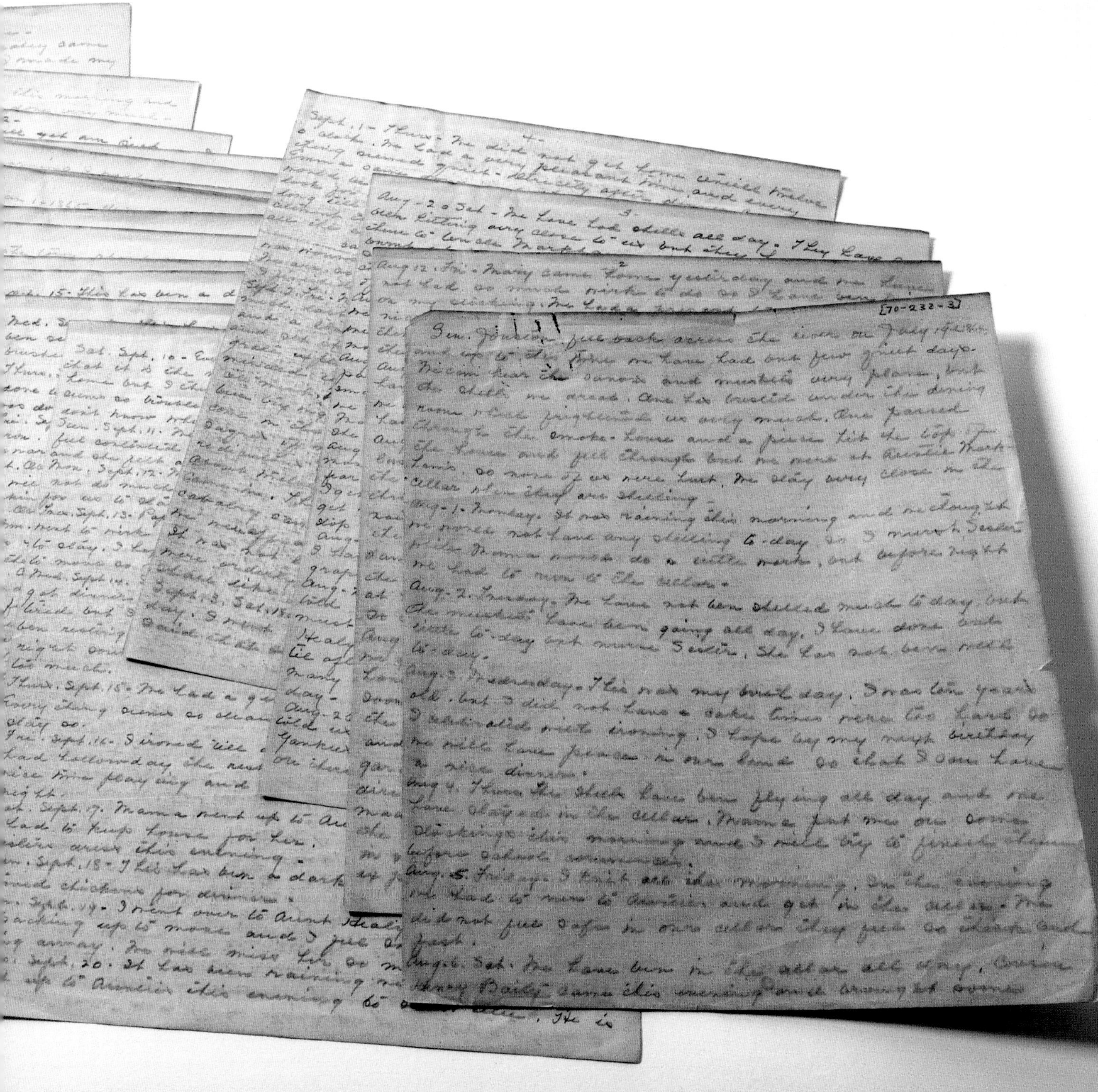

Wilbur Kurtz Easel

Artist Wilbur G. Kurtz described his career as his "adventures with Atlanta history." Using his skills as a painter and his passion for history, Kurtz's impact on recording Atlanta began with the many paintings and other works created on his easel.

A Midwestern transplant to the city, drawn to the South by his interest in the Civil War, Kurtz researched, documented, and illustrated the stories of old Atlanta. Through interviews with those who had lived through the Civil War and their descendants, explorations into the Georgia countryside, and close study of artifacts, Kurtz created paintings that showed Atlantans their history.

Kurtz's deep knowledge of Atlanta led Margaret Mitchell to ask for his help in fact-checking parts of her novel *Gone With the Wind*, and she also recommended him as the historian and technical adviser for its film adaptation.

In that role, Kurtz helped shape how generations imagined the Southern past, offering advice on a variety of details, including props, costumes, and set design. Though Kurtz strove for accuracy, he did not demand exact recreations and drama sometimes took precedence. As part of a Works Progress Administration project in the 1930s, Kurtz helped restore *The Battle of Atlanta* Cyclorama painting and oversaw the addition of diorama figures.

The Cyclorama is included as one of the other artifacts in *Atlanta in 100 Objects*.

Artist's Easel
Unidentified maker, circa 1950
Gift of Westville Historic Handicrafts, 1977

Jefferson Franklin Long

Born enslaved in central Georgia in 1836, Jefferson Franklin Long was Georgia's first Black representative in Congress when elected to office in 1870. National publications made note when Long, a successful tailor and businessman from Macon, took his seat in the House of Representatives. Comments in the press were largely limited to noting his race, describing him as a "Republican of African Descent."

Long also became the first Black representative to address the House of Representatives, opposing an amnesty bill that weakened the required federal loyalty oath to make it easier for former Confederates to serve in Congress. Nonetheless, the bill passed later that day by a vote of 118 to 90.

While in office, Long maintained an autograph book containing signatures of his fellow members of the 41st Congress, both senators and representatives, some of whom were also Black congressmen.

After the end of his term, Long did not hold public office again but remained a loyal member of the Republican Party. He was a delegate to the Republican National Conventions from 1872 to 1880, which nominated three successful Republican presidential candidates. As a businessman, he was respected in the Black community and earned a living sufficient to educate his six children.

A century passed before another Black person represented Georgia in Congress: Andrew Young, who was elected in 1972.

Lucinda Carhart and Jefferson Franklin Long
M.J. Lunquest's Gallery, Macon, circa 1859
Gift of Lucy Rucker Aiken, 1992

Congressional Autograph Book
Gift of Lucy Rucker Aiken, 1980

Marion, Bethune
Talbotton
Ga
1871
Jefferson F. Long
Macon Ga
1871

Grinding Stone

The earliest evidence of humans in the area of present-day Atlanta dates to approximately 13000 BCE with more permanent settlements appearing around 9000 BCE. Archaeologists separate the history of these people and their descendants into three cultural periods: Archaic (8000–1000 BCE), Woodland (1000 BCE–1000 CE), and Mississippian (800–1600 CE). Each is defined by changes in agricultural methods and tools.

Carved in the late Archaic era in the Soapstone Ridge southeast of Atlanta, grinding stones reflect the transition from a society of hunters to one of both hunters and gatherers. In addition to tools used to hunt and butcher animals, implements for processing food from plants were needed.

The Soapstone Ridge quarry, where people also lived and crafted tools like this grinding stone, was active from 3000 to 1000 BCE and continued into the Woodland period. This period saw improvements in agriculture, the development of pottery, and the establishment of permanent villages.

The craftspeople at Soapstone Ridge served more than their own community. Trading networks from the quarry extended south and west into present-day Florida and Louisiana, where people needed stone tools but lacked access to the quarries to make them.

Although named soapstone, the material from the quarry is meta pyroxenite, a type of igneous rock. Pyroxenite is a soft material that radiates heat, making it useful for cooking.

Grinding Stone
Meta pyroxenite,
circa 3000 BCE
Gift of Carolyn Cunningham, 1984

Priscilla and Percival
Rich's department store, Atlanta, 1953–1991
Gift of Rich's, 1996

Rich's Pink Pig

Measuring 16-feet long, the Pink Pig named Priscilla offered an unforgettable holiday experience for Atlanta's children.

Created in 1953 at Rich's department store in downtown Atlanta, the original ceiling monorail car circled high above the toy department. Eventually, the ride moved to the store's roof, where riders got a better view of Rich's other holiday tradition, the Great Tree. A visit to Rich's during the Christmas season to enjoy a ride on Priscilla, view the Great Tree, and dine at the Magnolia Room defined the holiday for many Atlantans.

Morris Rich, a German Jewish immigrant, opened a dry goods store in Atlanta in 1867. By 1901, the store evolved to become a true "department store" selling a variety of products to a growing middle class of consumers. The store's policies were unlike those of earlier dry goods stores. Items purchased could be returned without question or receipt, farmers were offered credit until their crops were harvested, and checks were cashed on Saturdays when banks were closed. In 1924, Rich's opened its flagship downtown Atlanta store on the corner of Alabama and Broad Streets.

As ownership and management of the store changed from the family-owned business to national chains, the connection to the community waned. In 2005, the use of Rich's as a store name ceased. Priscilla—and her sibling, Percival—remain as symbols of Rich's close connection to the city that it called home.

Confederate Ammunition Crate

On August 26, 1960, construction workers digging the roadbed for interstate highways I-75 and I-85 near downtown Atlanta uncovered one of the largest assortments of Confederate artifacts in Atlanta's history. It is known in local tradition as the "Expressway Cache."

Buried in the mud of a collapsed underground timber-and-earth supply depot were hundreds of Confederate artillery projectiles, muskets, railroad tools, and other military supplies. According to the *Atlanta Journal*, what followed was "a mad scramble" as workers, highway department employees, and curious onlookers looted the site and "hauled off their trophies."

Many of the unearthed artillery projectiles were 32-pounder spherical shells, probably made in Augusta, Georgia, or Selma, Alabama. The projectiles were still neatly packed in their original wooden shipping crates. This ammunition crate is so well preserved that a crude and misspelled shipping address is visible on one side: "To Gen'l Johnston / Atalanta [*sic*] / GA."

Because the site was not properly documented and excavated, we cannot know the extent of original artifacts or fully understand their historical significance. We do know, however, why it was there: located at the junction of four major railroads, Atlanta was the Confederacy's most important supply center. Its capture by Union Armies on September 2, 1864, put an end to the city's war-making capacity but not to its future importance as a modern "expressway" hub.

Confederate Ammunition Crate
Unidentified maker, 1864
Gift of Beverly M. DuBose III, 1995

Map of Azilia

While Europe bickered and rulers clashed, an Englishman named Sir Robert Montgomery was given a parcel of land from the Lords Proprietors of Carolina.

The year was 1717 and Montgomery, the fifth Scottish Baronet of Skelmorlie, quickly solicited funds to develop a settlement between British-occupied Carolina and the Spanish in Florida. He called the territory the Margravate of Azilia.

The word "margrave" is German and means a governor of a border province. In this case, Azilia was a buffer to prevent Spain's encroachment on British claims. To encourage investment, Montgomery set about writing glowing pamphlets on the beauty of the land and the possibilities of riches, including *The Most delightful Golden Islands: Being a Proposal for the Establishment of a Colony in the Country to the South of Carolina* in 1720.

By 1720, Montgomery had raised insufficient funding for the settlement and failed to secure royal approval. He relinquished his charter that year and died in 1731, just as James Oglethorpe was finalizing plans for settlement of the same land as the Province of Georgia.

Elements of Montgomery's failed margravate can be seen today. Montgomery's promotional tract named Georgia's barrier islands the Golden Isles. His extensive design for the unrealized capital of Azilia included multiple squares and a block layout. The plan would have been familiar to Oglethorpe and possibly influenced the layout of the city of Savannah.

→

Carolina nebst einem Theil von Florida

Herman Moll, geographer, 1729

Nuremberg: Homann Heirs, 1745

Purchase with funds from a bequest by Harvey M. Smith, 2025

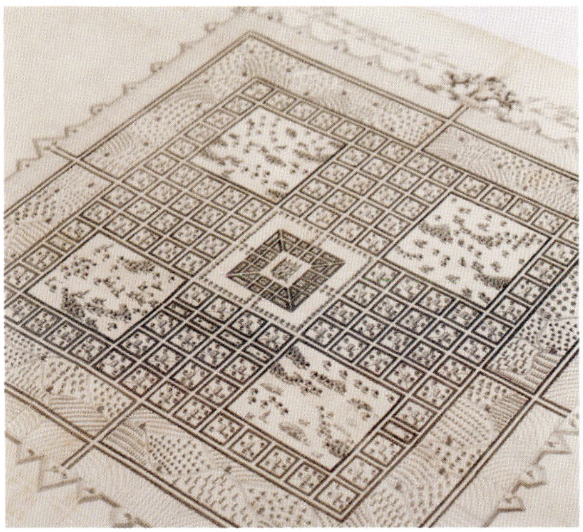

←

A Plan representing the Form of Settling the Districts, or County Divisions in the Margravate of Azilia

London: Sir Robert Montgomery, 1717

Purchase with funds from a bequest by Harvey M. Smith, 2025

OCEANUS
PARS AMERI-CÆ SEPTEN-TRIO-NALIS
NORD CARO-LINA
CAROLINA
AZILIA
Albemarl
Bath County
Claren-don County
Clarendon County
Craven County
Colletons County
Granville County
Charles Town
Port Royal
OCEANUS OCCIDENTAL

Ann Moore Couturiere

Fashion designer Ann Moore grew up in Atlanta. Seeing a playmate's "gorgeous" doll clothes, she learned they were handsewn by her friend. "I wanted to learn to sew like that," she says, "and that was my earliest inspiration to get into fashion." Graduating valedictorian from Booker T. Washington High School in 1938, Moore attended Spelman College, graduating in 1943.

Pursuing her fashion dream, Moore studied at New York's Traphagen School of Fashion—one of the nation's earliest fashion schools—and then at Fashion Academy, whose founder had inaugurated the first annual list of America's 10 best-dressed women in 1928.

In 1954, Moore attended École Guerre Lavigne in Paris. "I enrolled with an instructor who could not speak English," she recalls, "but he made his hands talk" when demonstrating the creative process of fashion draping. Moore connected with the Parisian aesthetic and philosophical approach to fashion design—haute couture.

In both New York and Paris, Moore was one of the first Black women to study professional fashion design. "My philosophy was each individual has a fashion persona," Moore says, "I find what that is and help you enhance that."

Living and designing in Detroit since the late 1940s, Moore established her own house of fashion, Ann Moore Couturiere, in 1963. Her collections appeared in *Jet*, *Vogue*, *Women's Wear Daily*, and other magazines and newspapers. After retiring and returning to Atlanta in 1982, Moore made a gift to Atlanta History Center of nearly 30 items that are—as praised by the *Detroit Free Press* in 1966—"timeless classics of quality and elegance."

Ann Moore Designs
Personal and commission designs, 1956–1967
Gift of Ann Moore Couturiere, 1992

Atlanta Daily World

As Auburn Avenue became the hub of Black life in Atlanta in the 1920s, W.A. Scott founded a newspaper, the *Atlanta Daily World*, in 1928. Scott wanted the newspaper "to inform and inspire and create jobs." With the vibrant Sweet Auburn neighborhood just outside the door, the newspaper was well positioned to report on the social, economic, and spiritual life of Black Atlantans.

On the two-mile stretch of Auburn Avenue just east of downtown, Black entrepreneurs and civic leaders created businesses, churches, and entertainment venues. Black Atlantans welcomed these spaces as an alternative to the deeply discriminatory Jim Crow environment elsewhere in Atlanta. Auburn Avenue business owners treated Black customers with dignity and courtesy.

These new businesses also offered uncommon job opportunities, as white employers typically limited Black workers to menial occupations. Entertainment venues attracted musical talent from around the nation. Historic churches, including Ebenezer Baptist Church, Big Bethel African Methodist Episcopal Church, and Wheat Street Baptist Church, formed the backbone of spiritual life for many Atlantans. National organizations, such as the NAACP, the Odd Fellows, and the Prince Hall Masons, maintained offices on the street.

The newspaper's name, *Atlanta Daily World*, reflects the mission of better informing Atlantans about both local life and the larger world at a time when white-owned newspapers largely ignored news related to Black life. By 1933, the newspaper had expanded and became a network serving 50 Black communities across the U.S. This teletype machine ensured the newspaper had the most current world news, connecting the paper to the UPI—United Press International—network of independent news.

Teletype Machine
United Press International, Washington, D.C., circa 1960
Gift of Alexis Scott, 1999

Atlanta National Bank Safe

In the fall of 1865, war-torn Atlanta needed a bank to finance the rebuilding of the city following the devastation of the Civil War. Chartered that September, the Atlanta National Bank was led by local merchant Alfred Austell. Until suitable quarters could be built, the bank set up operations in a spare room in Austell's home.

With the establishment of Atlanta National Bank, the city became the location of the first federally chartered bank in the former Confederacy. Codified by the National Banking Acts of 1863 and 1864, the new national banking system that allowed for federally chartered, privately owned banks was only a few years old.

The U.S. Congress passed these acts to help finance the Civil War. The acts would also lead to the adoption of a national currency, rather than both federal and state-issued notes. Congress authorized the issue of $60 million in notes that became known as "greenbacks," because the reverse side was printed in green.

Soon after opening for business, Atlanta National Bank informed the city council that it would be willing to lend Atlanta money to pay its bills. The city may have been very pleased to receive the information—Atlanta is said to have had $1.64 in funds after its surrender to Union forces in 1864.

The chartered bank helped Atlanta rebuild and prosper in the late 19th century. By 1929, after several bank acquisitions and charters, Atlanta National Bank was renamed the First National Bank of Atlanta and would be the largest bank in the South until the 1940s.

Bank Safe

Unidentified maker, circa 1865

Gift of Wachovia Bank of Georgia, 1991

Church Pulpit

This handmade pine pulpit once marked the center of worship for a Black community in rural South Georgia.

Following emancipation, Black Georgians were able to worship together freely in community congregations and churches. In an era when few people had large amounts of cash, church members donated materials and joined together to build new worship spaces. In spite of striking poverty, farmers pooled their resources, which led to a rapid increase in newly constructed churches across the state between 1865 and 1900.

The church was often the first structure built in a community other than homes, and many rural towns became known by the name of the church. Within the church, members achieved leadership roles denied to them in the larger, white-controlled society. Members also established mutual aid societies, sometimes called "sickness and burial societies," to help neighbors in need. Churches became the central social structure in rural areas.

For local families, church grounds offered space for schools, outdoor gatherings, and cemetery plots. The increase in Black literacy, from 5 percent in 1860 to 70 percent in 1900, reflects the efforts of Black communities to educate their children in schools that often met in rural churches. With few public funds available to support education for Black children, communities provided their own schoolrooms, furnishings, and more.

The crafting of this pulpit reflects the ways Black Georgians celebrated their new status as free Americans, building new lives and new communities of worship.

Church Pulpit
Unidentified maker,
circa 1880
Purchase with funds for the Folklife Collection, 1994

First Atlanta Air Mail Envelopes

On September 15, 1926, excitement was high at Atlanta's new airport, Candler Field. Thousands gathered to celebrate two aircraft headed in opposite directions. The southbound plane took off from Candler Field early in the morning, destined for Miami. The northbound plane, arriving from Miami, was scheduled to land in Atlanta at 3:50 p.m.

Appearing on schedule, the small plane circled the field to the sound of horns and whistles as it landed. Its major delivery was not passengers, but mail—air mail. The Florida Airways plane carried approximately 10,000 letters, 113 pounds in all.

The Florida plane was christened with a bottle of Chattahoochee River water and received a new name: *Miss Atlanta*. Nine months later, the route was discontinued because Florida Airways ceased all operations due to financial challenges. This was the end of air mail service to Atlanta until Pitcairn Aviation, later Eastern Air Lines, began deliveries in 1928.

Securing a mail route was integral to the success of early airlines. The government paid airlines per pound carried, and after 1930 payment was based on the space or volume available to carry mail on any given route. Combining income from both passengers and mail enabled airlines to grow their business and develop into a stable industry.

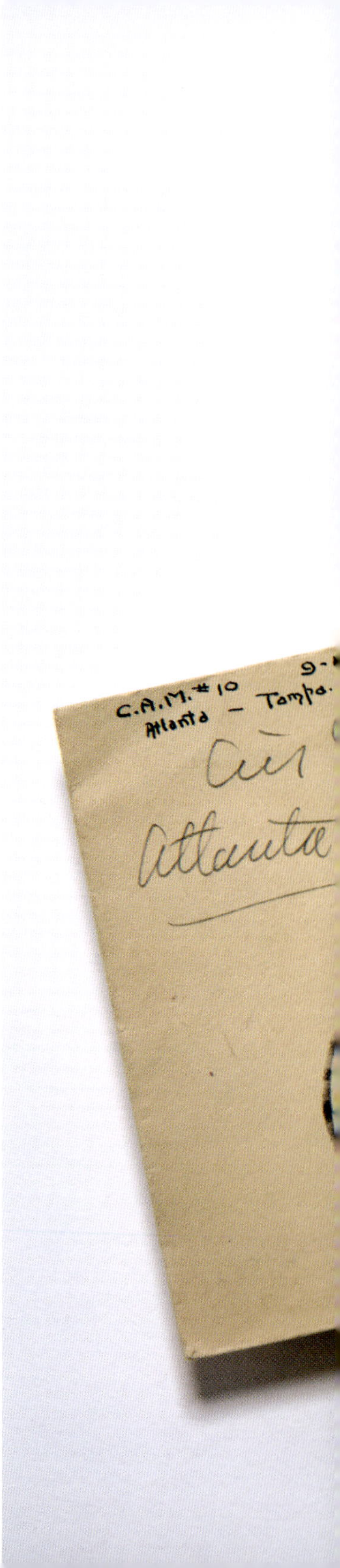

Air Mail Envelopes

Atlanta–Miami Route, September 15, 1926

Purchase with funds for the Collections, 2024

VIA AIR MAIL
UNITED STATES POSTAGE
AIR MAIL
10 CENTS 10
FIRST FLIGHT INAUGURATING CONTRACT AIR MAIL
MIAMI, FLA. 6:30 A. M. SEPT. 15, 1926
Mr. Lloyd B. Seal
303 Walton Building
Atlanta, Georgia
FIRST FLIGHT INAUGURATING CONTRACT AIR MAIL
ATLANTA, GA. 6:30 A. M. SEPT. 15. 1926
ATLANTA - MIAMI ROUTE

Backstreet Disco Ball

Located at 845 Peachtree Street in Midtown, Backstreet was a 24-hour dance club, bar, cabaret, and entertainment center comprising three levels and 10,000 square feet. First installed over the club's dance floor in 1977, this iconic disco ball, 4 feet in diameter and weighing nearly 100 pounds, oversaw 27 years of revelry.

In 2003, Backstreet was the only all-day bar left in the city, thus its motto: "Always Open and Always Pouring." When the city of Atlanta denied the annual renewal of the club's 24-hour liquor license, Backstreet closed when its license expired in 2004. The club transferred much of its interior and patrons, including this disco ball, to a bar off Cheshire Bridge Road called The Jungle. The Jungle remained there until development pushed it out of the leased space in 2017.

For many in the LGBTQ+ community, the disco ball represents more than the dancing and partying that are often associated with it. It also embodies the freedom and joy clubs like Backstreet brought LGBTQ+ people during a period of restricted rights and discrimination. In other dance clubs, bars, and some restaurants, gays and lesbians found safe spaces to build community, attain emotional support, and simply have the freedom to be themselves.

Under this disco ball, Atlanta's LGBTQ+ community and those from throughout the South found compassion, companionship, and love.

Disco Ball

Unidentified maker, circa 1977

Gift of Vicki Vara, 2017

AROLINA
LUMPKIN
HALL
FORSYTH
JACKSON
MADISON
CLARKE
GWINNETT
WALTON
MORGAN
DE KALB
NEWTON
HENRY
FAYETTE
BUTTS
AMPBELL
Marble Quarry
Canton
Social Hill
Roswell
Marietta
Warsaw
Pinckneyville
Cross Keys
Gibraltar
Stone Mt.
Yellow River
Lithonia
Decatur
Atlanta
Sand Town
Utoy
Campbellton
Fairburn
Jonesboro
Fayetteville
Stockbridge
White House
Mc Donough
Locust Grove
Conyers
Oxford
Covington
Emory College
Social Circle
Sheffield
Monroe
Cowpens
Chester
Newborn
Starrsville
Sandy Ridge
Double Cabins
Indian Springs
High Falls
Macon & W. R.R.

The First Georgia Map to Include Atlanta

Georgia's government faced a dilemma in the 1840s. The state's boundaries had changed rapidly following removal of the Muscogee and Cherokee tribes. The existing maps of Georgia were outdated and unreliable, making effective government challenging.

The state hired Milledgeville civil engineer William G. Bonner to draw the map. He was perfectly placed to get the job; Milledgeville was Georgia's capital at the time. Bonner gathered information for his work by studying previous maps and contacting the magistrates of newly formed counties. He used color to note county boundaries and included train tracks, waterways, and natural landmarks.

He even included a new Georgia city: Atlanta.

Atlanta had not been the first choice for the city's name. When founded in 1837, the site was unofficially known as Terminus because the settlement was at the terminal point of the Western & Atlantic Railroad. The town was incorporated as Marthasville in late 1843. The lengthy name was chosen in honor of Martha Lumpkin, whose father, politician and former governor of Georgia Wilson Lumpkin, advocated for the railroad and advised the street layout of the new city.

The name would change again when Georgia Railroad superintendent Richard Peters pointed out to his boss J. Edgar Thomson that Marthasville was too long to be printed on a single line of a railroad timetable. The two men invented a new name: Atlanta. The city's charter—as Atlanta—was approved in December 1847, and one month later the residents elected their first mayor, Moses Formwalt, representative of the Free and Rowdy Party.

Bonner's Pocket Map of the State of Georgia
Sherman & Smith, engravers, New York
Milledgeville, Georgia: William G. Bonner, 1848
Gift of Virginia Campbell Courts, 1970

The Locomotive *Texas*

Given Atlanta's establishment as a railroad hub, the 1856 locomotive *Texas* is perhaps the most significant historic object in the city.

In 1837, Atlanta was born when surveyor Stephen Harriman Long drove a stake into the ground at the point that would serve as the southern terminus of the yet-to-be-built rail line. This 4-4-0 American-type steam locomotive, constructed by Danforth, Cooke & Company, was ordered for the first railway in Atlanta, state-owned Western & Atlantic Railroad.

Today, the *Texas* is one of two surviving locomotives from the Western & Atlantic Railroad. The other is the *General*. Both were preserved because of their roles in Andrews' Raid on April 12, 1862. During that Civil War incident, Union spies stole a Confederate locomotive with the intent to destroy infrastructure deep inside Confederate territory. The thrilling episode, known as the Great Locomotive Chase, inspired two movies and resulted in the awarding of the first Medals of Honor in U.S. history.

Despite its starring role in the raid, the *Texas* hauled freight in obscurity for more than 40 years after the war. But for the efforts of railroad master mechanic H. Lamar Collier, artist Wilbur Kurtz, and the Ladies of Atlanta—an ad-hoc group—it would have been scrapped. The locomotive has been jointly displayed with the panoramic Cyclorama painting *The Battle of Atlanta* since 1911. The *Texas* was restored to its circa 1886 appearance and moved to Atlanta History Center in 2017 along with *The Battle of Atlanta* Cyclorama.

The *Texas*
Danforth, Cooke & Company, Paterson, New Jersey, 1856
Courtesy City of Atlanta, 2015

SOUTHERN RAILWAY
SR
REA EXPRESS
12
TEXAS
1936

GUDE-YATES
GOLF TROPHY
WON BY
ROBERT T. JONES JR.
JUNE 19TH 1919

Bobby Jones Golf Trophy

In 1930, Robert "Bobby" Tyre Jones Jr. achieved something no amateur golfer before or since has ever done—a "Grand Slam." In one year, he won the British Open, U.S. Open, British Amateur, and U.S. Amateur tournaments.

Jones was born in Atlanta in 1902 and his childhood home was next to the 13th hole on the newly built East Lake Golf Course. At the age of 14, he was the youngest competitor in the U.S. Amateur, although he didn't win it until he was 17. Jones chose to remain an amateur and retired from competitive golf at the age of 28 at the height of his career, just two months after completing the Grand Slam. His love of golf continued. After retirement, Jones published books on golf and spent time in Hollywood making instructional films about the sport.

With Clifford Roberts, he purchased Fruitland Nursery in Augusta, Georgia, in 1931 and built the Augusta National Golf Course. Designed by Jones and Scottish architect Alister MacKenzie, it remains a premier golf course, hosting the annual Masters Tournament, which Jones helped start.

This trophy, awarded to Jones in 1919 for winning the Gude-Yates Trophy Tournament, is named for Albert V. Gude, an Atlanta building contractor, and Presley Daniel Yates Sr., both members of the Atlanta Athletic Club. In 1938, Yates' son, Charles R. "Charlie" Yates, was himself an accomplished golfer, participating in many of the same tournaments as his friend and idol, Bobby Jones.

Gude-Yates Golf Trophy
Atlanta Athletic Club, East Lake Golf Club, 1919
Gift of Dr. and Mrs. William Arthur Smith, 1993

Regimental Flag of the 127th United States Colored Troops

This silk battle flag symbolizes the freedom struggle of Black soldiers during the Civil War, including some of the 462,000 people enslaved in Georgia as of 1860.

The United States Colored Troops (USCT) constituted a special branch of the U.S. Army formed after the Emancipation Proclamation of 1863. Three-fourths of the 180,000 soldiers in the USCT had been enslaved at one time.

USCT soldiers vowed to prove their worth by fighting for freedom and citizenship. Beneath the motto "WE WILL PROVE OURSELVES MEN," a soldier goes off to war while waving goodbye to Columbia, who symbolizes the United States. On the flag's reverse, an American bald eagle bears the national motto "E PLURIBUS UNUM," Latin for "Out of many, one."

This is one of three surviving examples of at least 12 USCT flags painted by Black artist David Bustill Bowser. He and his wife Elizabeth were leading organizers and contributors in the Philadelphia anti-slavery movement. Each of the original 12 flags cost $150.

The 127th USCT regiment trained at Camp William Penn near Philadelphia in 1864. The regiment flew this flag in combat during the Union Army's siege of Petersburg, Virginia, and at the April 1865 surrender of General Robert E. Lee and the Confederate Army of Northern Virginia at Appomattox Courthouse.

Regimental Flag
David Bustill Bowser, artist, Philadelphia, 1864
Purchase with funds from Sheffield-Harrold Charitable Trust, 2019

WE WILL PROVE OURSELVES MEN
127TH. REGT. U.S. COLORED TROOPS

Mayor William B. Hartsfield Chair

From 1937 to 1941 and again from 1942 to 1962, Atlanta Mayor William B. Hartsfield steered Atlanta through economic upheaval, civil rights reforms, and the construction of a major airport. Today, the airport—Hartsfield–Jackson Atlanta International Airport—bears his name along with that of another Atlanta mayor, Maynard Jackson.

Hartsfield was an early champion of the airport when he was a member of the city's Board of Aldermen. He advocated for the city to lease the former Atlanta Speedway in 1925 for use as an airport. Two years later, he supported the addition of lighting to keep the airport running day and night. By the end of Hartsfield's political career, the airport became one of the busiest in America.

His six terms and 23½ years in office witnessed incredible changes within the city. During that time, Atlanta's footprint grew from 37 to 128 square miles, and its population expanded from approximately 300,000 to 500,000 inhabitants. Hartsfield guided the city through the Great Depression by building a responsible budget that maintained Atlanta's city government through World War II.

Hartsfield supported a gradual approach to racial integration. He hired the city's first Black police officers in 1948 and informally engaged Black community leaders in political matters, giving them a voice often denied in official channels due to Jim Crow laws. Eventually, although civil rights activists rejected Hartsfield's indirect approach, his strategy may have helped Atlanta avoid racially charged violence seen in other Southern cities.

Desk Chair
Unidentified maker,
circa 1940
Gift of William C. Lusk, 2004

Carpetbag

Carpetbagger! Scalawag!

In the Reconstruction South in the decade following the Civil War, more disdainful words could not be found for "Yankees" in the South and for former white Confederates failing to act as expected. How did a colorful travel bag become such a symbol of derision and hate?

As the network of railways spread in the U.S. during the prewar period, trains were connecting people and places quickly and efficiently. As a result, a small industry developed to supply cheap travel bags. The bags were made from secondhand carpet scraps and sold for one or two dollars.

For Southerners after the Civil War, the bags came to symbolize outsiders—travelers from the North who came to the South to profit off the war; ravage local populations; and take advantage of efforts to rebuild the region's economy, politics, and social order.

In contrast, the term "scalawag" referred to a white Southerner who supported the federal government's Reconstruction program. That program included the unpopular terms for the political reintegration of former Confederate states into the U.S. Congress. It also included the establishment of civic and social equality for nearly four million recently freed African Americans.

Many white Southerners resisted changes that undermined the social fabric that had existed under the antebellum slave system and resented anyone who supported these policies—especially carpetbaggers and scalawags!

Carpetbag
Unidentified maker,
circa 1870
Gift of Mrs. Beverly M. DuBose Jr., 2008

Grand Army of the Republic Reunion Pot

This commemorative Boston bean pot was presented to Union Civil War veterans in Savannah by Union veterans from Beverly, Massachusetts. Three sides of the pot are adorned with the coats-of-arms of the states of Georgia and Massachusetts, as well as that of the Grand Army of the Republic, or GAR. Union veterans formed the GAR in 1866 to honor veterans' service through memorialization, charity, and political action.

The pot was given in gratitude for the care of the grave of a member of the Beverly veterans, Erastus B. Davis, who died in Georgia in 1887. Savannah veterans decorated his unmarked grave, pledging to "keep it in proper order and mount it with the flag for which he offered up his life."

The *Savannah Morning News* reported that the "comrades and friends of the departed heroes of the Union Army" performed annual rites at the graves of Davis and others. Graveside rituals included comments from a chaplain: "The blue and the gray . . . now lie side by side. All strife has been ended and only the olive branch prevails."

Commemorative Pot

C.A. Lawrence Pottery, Beverly, Massachusetts, 1890

Gift of Dean Day Sanders, 2022

Grady Hospital Nurse's Cape

In 1914, Ludie Clay Andrews, superintendent of the Black facilities at Atlanta's segregated Grady Hospital, opened the Grady Municipal Training School for Colored Nurses. The school won accreditation in 1917, and Andrews, after a court battle, became Georgia's first Black registered nurse in 1919.

Grady Memorial Hospital, named after Atlanta promoter and newspaper editor Henry W. Grady, had opened in 1892 with 100 beds and one operating room. Its mission was to "nurse the poor and rich alike" and "be an asylum for the black and the white." It remains Atlanta's public hospital and today has nearly 1,000 beds.

Ludie Andrews' first class of nursing students passed their exams in 1920 and began assisting in the newly created J.J. Gray outpatient clinic for Black patients. In 1921, an Atlanta Medical College building was converted to a hospital to care for African American patients. The term "the Gradys" was coined to express the separate wards, clinics, and hospitals offered to Black and white patients.

In 1964, Grady's nursing schools were integrated and the hospital followed one year later. The nursing program ceased operations in 1982, but medical training continues at Grady Hospital, which is internationally recognized as a teaching hospital. Students and residents from Emory University School of Medicine and Morehouse School of Medicine train at Grady.

Nurse's Uniform Cape
C.E. Ward Company,
New London, Ohio,
circa 1941
Gift of Juanita Yates Harrell, 1994

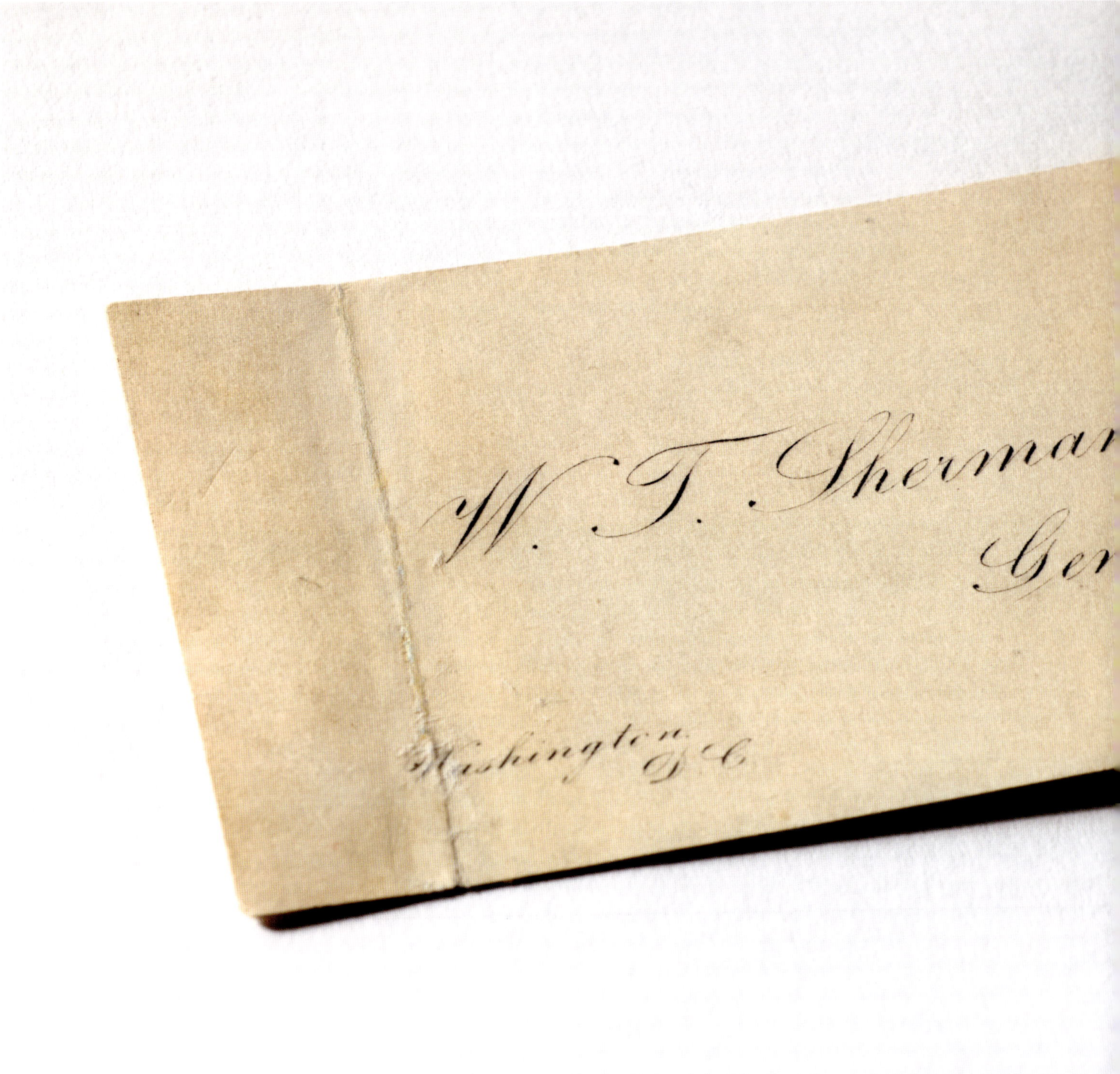
W. T. Sherman
Washington D.C.

Sherman's Calling Card

In January 1879, General William T. Sherman returned to Atlanta, calling cards in hand, to meet leaders of the city he had devastated 15 years before during the Civil War. In a visit very different from his arrival in 1864, Sherman received a warm welcome. Atlantans gathered at the train station to welcome the Commanding General of the United States Army, with only the occasional sly comment about fire.

Over three days, Sherman met with local and state officials, including then Georgia Governor Alfred H. Colquitt and Joseph E. Brown, the governor during the Civil War. In a meeting with Mayor William Calhoun, onlookers reported that Sherman heaped praise on Calhoun's father, James Calhoun, who had been mayor of Atlanta during the war and had surrendered the city to the Union Army. Sherman left the current mayor beaming with pleasure.

Calling Card
Unidentified printer, circa 1879
Gift of the Calhoun Family, 1939

Dr. Benjamin Mays to Mayor Ivan Allen Jr.

Dr. Benjamin Mays, president of Morehouse College and a civil rights activist, sent a letter of thanks to Mayor Ivan Allen Jr. in July of 1963 following Allen's appearance before the U.S. Senate Commerce Committee.

Allen had traveled to Washington to support a proposed law that would require hotels, restaurants, and other public accommodations to desegregate their facilities and serve Black as well as white customers. In his testimony, Allen told the senators of his personal experience seeking voluntary change in Atlanta. He stated that businesspeople wanted federal government involvement to provide cover for desegregation. He asked Congress, "give us some direction, give us some definition" to discourage those who had agreed to desegregate from backing down.

Allen predicted his testimony would make his reelection as mayor unlikely. In this letter, an optimistic Mays suggested the testimony was not "political suicide." Other messages to Allen reflected divided public opinion. Allen received venomous unsigned postcards as well as telegrams of thanks and letters with warm praise for his courage.

Two years later, Allen won a decisive victory with 70 percent of the vote. While 51 percent of white voters supported Allen, the strong support from Black voters ensured victory. Allen's accomplishments during his eight years as mayor include a downtown building boom, population growth of 30 percent, construction of major highways, and the arrival of major league sports in the city.

Dr. Benjamin E. Mays to Mayor Ivan Allen Jr.
July 29, 1963
Courtesy City of Atlanta, 2014

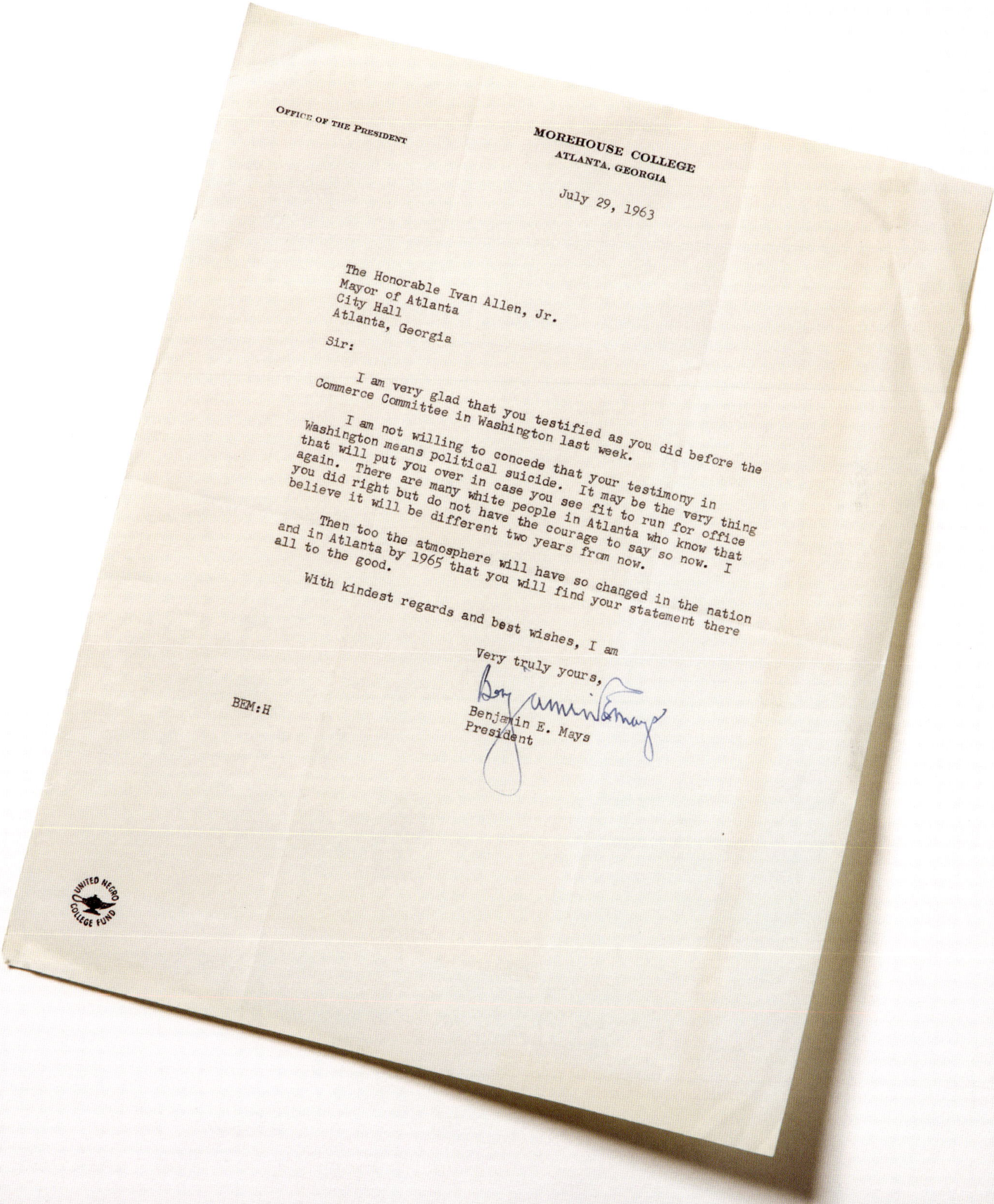

OFFICE OF THE PRESIDENT

MOREHOUSE COLLEGE
ATLANTA, GEORGIA

July 29, 1963

The Honorable Ivan Allen, Jr.
Mayor of Atlanta
City Hall
Atlanta, Georgia

Sir:

I am very glad that you testified as you did before the Commerce Committee in Washington last week.

I am not willing to concede that your testimony in Washington means political suicide. It may be the very thing that will put you over in case you see fit to run for office again. There are many white people in Atlanta who know that you did right but do not have the courage to say so now. I believe it will be different two years from now.

Then too the atmosphere will have so changed in the nation and in Atlanta by 1965 that you will find your statement there all to the good.

With kindest regards and best wishes, I am

Very truly yours,

Benjamin E. Mays
President

BEM:H

UNITED NEGRO COLLEGE FUND

The Weavers of Rabun

In 1934, Mary Crovatt Hambidge founded the Weavers of Rabun, a studio in Rabun County, Georgia. There, the unlikely connection between traditional craft skills of North Georgia women and those of Greece led to the creation of elegant fabrics and garments.

Following a childhood in Georgia, Hambidge moved to the Northeast for her education and to work as an actress. On a trip to Greece with her husband, Jay Hambidge, in 1919, she apprenticed with traditional weavers. She returned to the U.S. with a loom and a love of weaving. After her husband's death in 1924, Hambidge settled near Rabun Gap in northeast Georgia and founded a weaving studio on the banks of Betty's Creek.

Hambidge recruited local women to spin and weave, including older women who had learned to spin from their grandmothers and younger women she trained. The women welcomed the income, often from jobs they completed at home. The weavers used natural materials: thread spun from silk, cotton, and wool from the sheep that grazed in the fields surrounding the studio. Hambidge tinted fabrics with colors inspired by nature with the subtle tones of flower blossoms, plants, and autumn leaves.

The hours of intricate handwork created beautiful fabrics priced more for wealthy Northeasterners—they were sold at a shop on New York City's Madison Avenue —than rural Georgians. In 1948, shoppers on Peachtree Street enjoyed a rare chance to learn about the Georgia-made textiles. Crowds gathered at the windows of Davison's department store to see 80-year-old Flora Norton demonstrate the art of spinning.

As of 2025, the Hambidge Center continues operation by sponsoring residencies, workshops, and opportunities for creative exchange. The center is listed on the National Register of Historic Places.

Hambidge Designs

Mary Crovatt Hambidge, designer and weaver, Rabun Gap, Georgia, 1924–1928

Purchase with funds for the Hambidge Collection, 1998

Mayor Maynard Jackson

The Great Speckled Bird was an alternative weekly Atlanta newspaper published between 1968 and 1976. The paper had a reputation for skewering the stodgy status quo at all levels of government. Covering the election of Maynard Jackson, Atlanta's first Black mayor, in 1973, the newspaper tried to balance its typical critique of authority with the possibility of change.

When Jackson was elected, he was aware of the pressure put on "firsts" by Atlantans Black and white. Criticism that he was moving too fast or too slow, taking on too much or too little continued throughout his three terms in office. Referring to himself as a "transition" mayor, Jackson hoped to make the city more equitable for Atlanta's minorities and demonstrate his ability to manage a large city administration.

One of Jackson's proudest achievements was the construction of a new airport terminal for Atlanta, a project that contracted more minority and women-owned businesses than had previous major undertakings. After construction of the terminal concluded, he was able to say, "We built the Atlanta Airport, the biggest terminal building complex in the world, ahead of schedule and within budget."

After his death in 2003, Jackson's name was added to the airport, which was then named for former Mayor William B. Hartsfield, an early advocate for an airport in the 1920s. The name, Hartsfield–Jackson Atlanta International Airport, connects two pivotal eras of Atlanta's history.

The Great Speckled Bird
Atlanta: Atlanta Cooperative News Project, October 22, 1973
Atlanta Newspaper Collection, 1973

GREAT SPECKLED
The BIRD
ALTERNATIVE MEDIA SHARED BY 50,000 PEOPLE IN ATLANTA, THE SOUTH AND THE NATION
Copyright/Atlanta Cooperative News Project Volume Six Number Forty One October 22, 1973
OLD POLITICS NEW TWIST
JACKSON FOWLER TEAM ELECTED

6 1/2 FL. OZ.

Coca-Cola Bottle

At the turn of the 20th century, the Coca-Cola Company faced both challenges and opportunities. Under the leadership of Asa Candler Sr., the company worked to balance its complicated relationship with the patent-medicine industry with the business opportunities presented by a new century thirsty for a tasty, refreshing beverage. Already popular, the beverage had the potential to grow even more.

In 1899, Joseph Whitehead and Benjamin Thomas of Chattanooga, Tennessee, approached Candler with a business proposition: Why not bottle Coca-Cola?

Candler was reluctant at first, fearing that the quality of the beverage might suffer. He had good reason to be concerned. Following his approval, Whitehead and Thomas started their first bottling operation in Chattanooga, a humble affair that revealed a limitation of the bottle design: It led to spoilage quickly, giving the beverage a shelf life of only 10 days in hot weather—a real hazard in the South.

Whitehead and Thomas evolved the company into a franchise model with Whitehead bringing in John Thompson Lupton to help fund the first bottling plant in Atlanta. Innovations in bottle and bottle-cap design helped solve quality-control issues and led to an explosion of bottling companies opened under the umbrella of the company headquartered in Atlanta. By 1909, there were 397 Coca-Cola bottling companies in the U.S.

No longer restricted to a soda fountain, consumers enjoyed the beverage when and where they wanted. The innovation was a great success. John Thompson Lupton's grandson sold the family business back to Coca-Cola Company in 1986 for approximately $1.4 billion. In 1899, the bottling company had paid one dollar for the right to bottle Coca-Cola.

Coca-Cola Bottle
Coca-Cola Bottling Company, Atlanta, circa 1900
Gift of Donald R. Rooney, 2015

World War I Uniform

In August 1918, Atlanta-born Wilhemina Drummond sailed for Europe to support the Allied war effort. On her 5-foot-1-inch frame, this trim uniform marked her as a member of the Red Cross Motor Corps, working as a mechanic and ambulance driver.

Drummond's service reflected the new roles that became available to women during World War I. While women could not vote or serve in combat, many embraced support roles. New technology, including automobiles, changed warfare. Women who knew how to drive were in demand for transporting patients, delivering medical supplies, and braving artillery fire to retrieve wounded soldiers.

In Atlanta, women formed the Georgia Division of the Woman's Committee of the Council of National Defense. The group organized statewide support, including advocating for food conservation, working with soldiers' families, and selling Liberty Bonds.

Drummond's work in Europe began in an ambulance unit attached to the Sixth French Army. Later, in Serbia, she led the transportation program of the Virginia Hospital Unit. In 1920, Drummond returned to Georgia with multiple medals from both France and Serbia, and with memories of challenging tasks like riding a boxcar through Greece to deliver 300 hospital beds for a Serbian medical unit.

In 1922, Drummond married businessman John Harland. Her life as Mrs. Harland included community leadership roles, motherhood, and, with her husband, supporting Atlanta philanthropies. As the nation rallied to support troops during World War II, Mrs. Harland returned to service in the Red Cross Motor Corps, this time serving on the home front by managing transportation for the servicemen passing through Atlanta's Terminal Station.

Woman's Uniform
Abercrombie & Fitch,
New York, 1918
Gift of Mrs. John A. Conant, 1978

Boar's Head Soup Tureens

In 1982, Atlanta History Center received a generous bequest from Philip Trammell Shutze, the architect of Swan House located on the organization's campus.

> During my lifetime, I have collected items of decorative arts that mean a great deal to me. I wish to bequeath this collection to assure its continued preservation, maintenance, and enjoyment—and display the collection in Swan House, which was designed by me.

Celebrated for his architecture, Shutze was also an enthusiastic, talented, and determined collector. Between 1949 and 1953, he assembled a collection of silver, paintings, and textiles, and as many as 100 pieces of antique English and American furniture, all dating from the late 18th and early 19th centuries. Shutze's passion, however, was ceramics, primarily Chinese and English porcelain and pottery, and he collected nearly 700 such objects.

The most celebrated and rare work in his collection is this pair of boar's head tureens, based on an original from Strasbourg, France. Chinese porcelain factories copied the tureen for export to the European market, where animal forms were fashionable in the mid-18th century. The tureen is documented in Dutch East India Company records, noting that 25 boar's head tureens were purchased in 1763 and 19 more in 1764. There are no other boar's head tureen orders.

Shutze lived with and enjoyed his collection on a daily basis, rather than simply maintaining it for display. He used these tureens for Thanksgiving dinner, with the steam from the hot soup rising from the nostrils of the boar.

Soup Tureens
Chinese Export porcelain, 1763–1764
Bequest of Philip Trammell Shutze, 1982

ATLANTA
INFLUENCES
EVERYTHING

Atlanta Influences Everything Hoodie

In 2015, Atlanta native and community culture curator Bem Joiner was upset when he discovered that Nike athletic wear would not include Atlanta in a campaign highly influenced by the city's dominant hip-hop culture. His frustration led Joiner to coin the phrase "Atlanta Influences Everything." Printed on T-shirts, hoodies, and hats, it allows Atlantans to show the pride they have in a city that is taking a lead in the 21st century.

Joiner and his two co-founders, Ian Ford and Tory Edwards, were creating more than just a slogan with Atlanta Influences Everything (AIE). They were attempting to organize and connect Atlanta's growing creative class with projects and funders in the city. AIE is "focused on combining civic, corporate, and cultural understanding to harness the influence of Atlanta culture to do good and connect communities."

For those who study the history of Atlanta, a more apt slogan may not be possible. Atlanta was the site of the crucial Union victory that secured Abraham Lincoln's 1864 presidential reelection and the eventual end of the Civil War. It was the setting of Margaret Mitchell's best-selling novel *Gone With the Wind* and its movie version, which set box office records and spurred a slew of cultural tributes, including neighborhood names, questionable suburban architecture, and high-profile television satires.

Atlanta businesses, including Coca-Cola and Delta Air Lines, are global icons. The Civil Rights Movement found a home in Atlanta and the words of the Rev. Dr. Martin Luther King Jr. continue to inspire opposition to injustice throughout the world. Since the middle of the 1990s, hip-hop and pop music has been filtered heavily through Atlanta musicians and producers.

Atlanta Influences Everything because it's impossible to imagine a world without it.

Hoodie
Champion, Winston-Salem, North Carolina, 2024
Gift of Atlanta Influences Everything, 2025

Future Atlanta Campaign Donors*

Atlanta History Center is grateful to donors who contributed to the Future Atlanta Centennial Capital Campaign.
*Gifts and pledges received as of September 26th, 2025

Foundations & Corporations

A Friend of Atlanta History Center
Anonymous
Anonymous
The Thomas and Spring Savitt Asher Foundation
Atlanta Foundation
The Coca-Cola Foundation
Connolly Family Foundation
Courts Foundation
The James M. Cox Foundation
The Frances and Beverly DuBose Foundation
The Fraser-Parker Foundation
Georgia Power Foundation
The Wilbur & Hilda Glenn Family Foundation
The Goizueta Foundation
Hills Family Foundation
The Imlay Foundation
The Louise H. and David S. Ingalls Foundation
Kelin Foundation
The Ma-Ran Foundation
D. Lurton Massee Community Welfare Fund
Morgens West Foundation
Norfolk Southern
The Rich's Foundation
The Gary W. Rollins Foundation
Sartain Lanier Family Foundation
The Sheffield-Harrold Charitable Trust
Truist Trusteed Foundations: Florence C. and Harry L. English Memorial Fund
Tull Charitable Foundation
Robert W. Woodruff Foundation
The Zeist Foundation

Individuals

Juliet and John Allan
Angie and Sam Allen
The Beaumont Allen Family
Juliet Asher and Michael Golden
Chloe Barzey and Ralph Donaldson, Jr.
Jill Campbell Bullock and George Bullock
Anna and Dallas Clement
Linda Copeland
Jennifer Dorian and James Graham Dorian
Allison and Billy Dukes
Florida and Doug Ellis
Dr. Corinne Erickson and Will Skeean
Katie and Reade Fahs
Patrice and Ernest Greer
Stephanie and Marc Hardy
Joia M. Johnson Legacy Fund
Trudy and Doug Kremer
Jim Landon
The Langley Family
Libby and David Lanier
Kelly Loeffler and Jeff Sprecher
Jackie and Tony Montag
Sandra Hall Mulrain
Victoria and Howard Palefsky
Marianna and Solon Patterson
Carey and Bill Peard
Rebecca and Ralph Morrison
Neva and Don Rountree
Lovette and Michael Russell
The Shailendra Family
Lynn and Bill Shearer
Caroline Rawls Strumph and Matthew Strumph
Charles Turner
Kathy N. Waller and Kenneth Goggins
Anne Glenn Weltner
Betsy and Mark West

Contributors

Research and Writing
Amy Durrell and Lisa Flaherty

Timothy Frilingos, Gordon Jones, Jackson McQuigg, and Michael Rose

Editorial Support
Claire Haley, Lucy Abell, and John Schmidt

Photography
All photography by Mark Hill Photography except as noted below.

Atlanta History Center: pp. 103, 104 bottom, 105, 114.

Sarah Carter: pp. 6–7, 104 bottom.

Jason Hales Photography: pp. 92–92, 106–11, 174–75.

Jena Jones: p. 33.

Jack W. Melton Jr. Photography: pp. 182–83.

Nick Ozorak: pp. 178–79.

Michael Rose: pp. 102, 104 top.

Rod Smith: pp. 32, 90–91, 113, 132–33, 142–43, 162–63, 164–65, 166–67, 194–95.

Digital Services
Jena Jones

Project Manager
Timothy Frilingos

Publication Manager
Michael Rose

Chief Content Officer
Pola Changnon

First published in 2026 by
Scala Arts Publishers, Inc.
c/o CohnReznick LLP
10th floor, 1301 Avenue of the Americas
New York, NY 10019, USA
www.scalapublishers.com
An imprint of B. T. Batsford Holdings Ltd.

In association with Atlanta History Center

ISBN 978-1-78551-625-2
A Library of Congress Control Number is available for this publication
Edited by Susan Higman Larsen
Designed by Eoghan O'Brien and Juliette Clark
Printed in China

Scala is represented in the UK and Europe by Abrams & Chronicle Books, 1st Floor, 22–24 Ely Place, London, EC1N 6TE and 57 rue Gaston Tessier, 75166 Paris, France.

10 9 8 7 6 5 4 3 2 1

Photographic credits
All photography by Mark Hill Photography except as noted below.

Atlanta History Center: pp. 103, 104 bottom, 105, 114. Sarah Carter: pp. 6–7, 104 bottom. Jason Hales Photography: pp. 92–92, 106–11, 174–75. Jena Jones: p. 33. Jack W. Melton Jr. Photography: pp. 182–83. Nick Ozorak: pp. 178–79. Michael Rose: pp. 102, 104 top. Rod Smith: pp. 32, 90–91, 113, 132–33, 142–43, 162–63, 164–65, 166–67, 194–95.